Knowing Woman

2-24-09

Love + Blessings

Jo Garceau

PRAISE FOR

JO GARCEAU
and
KNOWING WOMAN

"Women live in a different world today because of the author and her pioneering work in 'women's rights', as well as in her spiritual quest. A must read."

~Ralph Munro, Secretary of State, Washington State

"If we are instruments of God, then Jo Garceau's work is an orchestra. Readers, regardless of where they are on their spiritual journey, will find this book enlightening and very informational. It's a must read for anyone on their personal quest. Two more words...life changing".

~ Jeff Elkins, Sound Therapist/healer/photo-journalist

"A fascinating account of a woman's courageous journey to self knowledge"

~ Janet D'Urso, author of *The Social Construction of Woman*, Melbourne, Australia

"In these times of deep division, Jo Garceau offers a path toward wholeness. Hers is a remarkable pilgrimage, both feminist and spiritual, of learning to integrate her self with the world."

~Joanne Mulcahy, Northwest Writing Institute, Lewis and Clark College; author of *Birth and Rebirth on An Alaskan Island*

"...wonderfully expressive writing style! Great color and creativity. ...makes me want to read more. Vivid."

~Fred Rozendal, pyschotherapist, San Francisco

"A thoughtful, stimulating account of the inner workings of a dynamic state office and very popular governor, from the viewpoint of an insightful administrator, this is an important account of a very critical period in Washington state history. It would be a valuable read for anyone planning a public service career. The spiritual side, often neglected by other comparable writers, provides a true bonus."

~Roger Meyer MD Clinical Professor of Pediatrics and Public Health, University of Washington; President, Child and Family Health Foundation.

"I have known Jo Garceau for over 38 years. She has been an asset in developing wisdom and clarity. Her book will be a welcomed addition to understanding how we can better relate to God and each other."

~Paul R Meyer, Seattle King County Ombudsman

"If you have a room of your own, go there and read *Knowing Woman*. If you don't yet have such a place, find a quiet public location and read this book, then set out to create conditions in your life to tell your story in your own way by the light of this one."

~Kim Stafford, author of *The Muses Among Us*, Director, Northwest Writing Institute

Knowing Woman

✦

Nurturing the Feminine Soul

Jo Mills Garceau

iUniverse, Inc.
New York   Bloomington

Knowing Woman
Nurturing the Feminine Soul

iUniverse books may be ordered through booksellers or by contacting:

iUniverse
1663 Liberty Drive
Bloomington, IN 47403
www.iuniverse.com
1-800-Authors (1-800-288-4677)

ISBN: 978-0-595-47269-7 (pbk)
ISBN: 978-0-595-91545-3 (ebk)
ISBN: 978-0-595-71932-7 (cloth)

Printed in the United States of America

iUniverse rev. date: 10/23/2008

For my children:
Paul, Suzanne, Warren, and Gregory

Contents

Foreword

My campaign for governor in 1964 was a campaign of volunteers. We raised money, ran ads, and used television, but it was our army of volunteers who won the race. Jo Garceau was one of those remarkable campaigners who gave extraordinary amounts of time and talent for no pay except the reward of victory.

A few years later, Jo came to work in the governor's office. She quickly showed unusual skills and I asked her to take on a difficult responsibility. In my early years as governor, I found to my dismay that I was responsible for appointing citizens to hundreds of boards and commissions as well as making judicial appointments when vacancies occurred. I knew this offered a real opportunity to expand participation of women and minorities in policymaking positions, but we had no rational process to make selections.

I said, "Jo, make some sense out of this jumble of laws and regulations and help me broaden opportunity for women and minorities in state government." It was one of my best decisions. Over the next few years, Jo created a cohesive system of pending vacancies and lists of outstanding candidates to fill those positions. Soon we had vibrant, active citizen commissions giving me and department heads innovative ideas that help made state government better.

As I began my third term as governor, I was determined to bring citizens even more closely into policymaking. I initiated Alternatives for Washington and asked Jo Garceau to select a broad cross-section of Washingtonians to begin this effort. Soon, she was deeply involved in what became a remarkable experience of participatory democracy. Hundreds of selected volunteers devised eleven potential alternatives for Washington's future. These were distributed to all citizens in a tabloid insert in every newspaper in the state. We were overwhelmed with 60,000 replies choosing their favorite alternative and usually writing extensive letters in addition.

Soon, communities around the state were creating their own programs and citizen activism was in full flower. Jo was at the center of all of this and we were both disappointed when my time as governor ended and we were unable to continue this remarkable program.

But this book is not just about a lifetime of activity. It, instead, is a remarkable story of a search for faith and the true meaning of life. Each step of that search opened new opportunities for Jo to grow intellectually and to contribute remarkably to the community around her.

I was blessed to have her share a portion of that contribution to me and the citizens of Washington through her pacesetting efforts in the governor's office.

Daniel J. Evans
Governor, Washington 1965–1977

Acknowledgments

This book has been a long time in the making, from when I first began journaling in 1960, to 1991 when I purchased a computer and began shaping a book, to the present.

I wish to thank all my friends and teachers in writing classes at Marylhurst University, Lewis and Clark College, and Mt. Hood Community College for the opportunity to learn and share with so many creative people. I particularly acknowledge the gifted teaching of Kim Stafford and Joanne Mulcahy of the Northwest Writing Institute who taught me to trust my creative flow. Thanks, too, to Joan Maiers of Marylhurst University for the line-by-line edit we conducted over two semesters.

And a shout of pleasure to Elizabeth Udall and the Walden Fellowship for the six-week Writing Fellowship retreat in Gold Hill, Oregon, in 1998. While only one chapter in the book reflects that special time, the retreat was a confidence-building gift that could never be duplicated.

Special thanks to my sister Helen Louisa Dupuis for her insightful suggestions in the beginning and middle stages of writing this spiritual memoir. Especially to my sisters Lucille, Carol, and Loretta, I offer appreciation for encouraging me.

Without the loving support of my friends and fellow readers at Celestial Awakenings this past two years, especially owners Angela Anno, Betty and Jimmy Masure, and Kim and Jeff Elkins, I might never have completed the book. Thank you, Daniel Giamario, my astrological mentor and celestial friend for your knowledge and guidance.

I am eternally grateful to Rob Layman for the cover photo.

Thanks to Cindy Bridge who read the next-to-last version of *Knowing Woman* and offered an entirely new perspective. Blessings, Cindy.

A huge hug and thanks to my sister Liz Barker who told me she couldn't wait to read and share my writing with her reading group in Anchorage, Alaska, thus planting the seed for reshaping the book so that each reader might nourish her/his own soul.

And finally, to Greg, who is always there for me, a huge mother's hug.

Introduction

From as early as I can remember, I lived a façade. As a girl and later a woman, I pretended to be what I perceived other people expected me to be.

Yet, at eight, when my soul—my spiritual self—first made itself known, an inner voice insisted I would be different from any woman I had ever heard of. This both mystified and challenged me, for it was in direct conflict with convention.

In the 1930s world I grew up in, women were subsidiary to men. Church, family, and society taught only one way for a girl to grow up—the way her mother, grandmother, and every woman who lived before her had. Dependent on men for status and economic support, we were expected to be beautiful and compliant, never independent in thought or manner. When our beauty faded, our worth dissipated. Taught this way for millennia, women were objects of scorn and derision, barely second-class citizens. Why, in the United States, only a decade before my birth, women were finally allowed to vote!

For six decades, even though my natal astrological chart indicates an independent woman, strong and courageous with a keen interest in politics, psychology, and spirituality, chronic depression was my constant companion. Until I realized the life purpose I had heard as a child emanated from my feminine soul, my heart was hollow at the center. I ached with emptiness. Awareness came slowly and incrementally—a spiral journey toward self-understanding, driven by an inner mandate, punctuated by tiny, seemingly insignificant but ultimately life-changing decisions.

From that secret soul announcement of my life mission at eight years of age, to the full blossoming of a life centered in the Self—slowly the Divine Feminine became a fountain of harmony, peace, and tranquility.

Thirty-five years ago, Jungian analyst Irene Claremont de Castillejo, in her popular book of the time, *Knowing Woman, A Feminine Psychology*, asked her readers to join in the effort to bring the souls of women from the dark underground cavern where they had hidden for centuries up into the light of consciousness. I was immensely struck with her description of the ways women develop and her call for an authentic feminine psychology.

Psychology of Women

Depth psychology, introduced by Sigmund Freud and Carl Jung in the late nineteenth and early twentieth centuries, pioneered the idea of unconscious aspects of human consciousness. In this model, much of human thought and action is culturally and/or personally repressed because it is deemed unacceptable. Since the culture historically placed women in a secondary role to men, who women were in their natural state was buried deep in the psyche, in the unconscious. The psychology of women recognizes this cultural inhibition and encourages women to express their personal truth.

In the latter decades of the twentieth century, women psychologists, often trained by Carl Jung, began to posit an authentic feminine psychology, different from the psychological makeup of men.

Reading and rereading her words, I formed the desire to help uncover the feminine soul and dreamed of joining with many other women in this important psychological work. I wanted every woman to become aware of her higher self, her soul, to be inspired to make her personal journey. I decided to try to find my inner self so that I could share what I found.

Levels of Self/Ego

The persona, one's way of meeting the world, is separate from the little self or ego, the collection of traits, desires, and beliefs forming the entirety of the personality. The soul/higher self is the essence of an individual, that part of the individual that was before birth and remains after the body dies. When a person becomes self-realized (i.e., spiritually enlightened), the soul self expands into the entirety of creation, becomes the entirety, known as the greater Self/God. Thus, coming to know one's spiritual self (in Hindi, the *atman*) ultimately can bring one to realization that who one is is one with the entirety of all creation. Paramahansa Yogananda, author of *The Autobiography of a Yogi*, sang, "I am a bubble, make me the sea." In other words, I am the little self, make me the big Self, one with God.

By the time I read Irene de Castillejo, I had married, borne four children, become a feminist politician and a Catholic Charismatic. As my search for the feminine soul accelerated and became the focus of my life, I became an ecumenical campus minister. Later, I joined a Hindu-Christian ashram, went on pilgrimage to Israel and India, and on a Vision Quest. Eventually, I came to the awareness that my soul relates to Great Mystery without religious structures. That story is reflected in the narrative, the first and major part of this book.

From the vantage point of seventy-five years lived, I view the seemingly inexhaustible ways that the soul operates. I came into this life with a soul agenda—all of us do. For most of my years, my conscious mind thought it was fully in charge. Around the time of my fiftieth birthday, I began to question that. Today, my ego still makes day-to-day decisions, but I believe the soul intervenes when I lose the direction it intends.

My soul has guided me in countless ways. First, there was a voice; later, a telegraphed message and countless synchronous events.

My soul often expressed itself to me through nature—shooting stars, a small local earthquake, animal signs, a limpet shell, a magnificent sunset, and a feminine, double terminated healing crystal. Each played an important role in my life.

There were visions, meditations, glossolalia, and kundalini. Messages—some encouraging, others devastatingly challenging—came through others; the challenging illness of my youngest child has taught me more than almost any other life experience. Inspired by my soul, I followed my intuitions and learned astrology. Dreams guided me. Spiritual light permeated my being, and joy held me spellbound. At times, I failed miserably; at other times, doors opened effortlessly.

Contrary to the popular belief that soul experiences are irrational, unexplainable, and therefore unreal, I believe soul messages, in whatever form, are the heart and truth of who we are. I am convinced that everyone experiences the soul/Self, not necessarily as I experience it, but in manifold ways. We are first and foremost souls with bodies and minds, not the other way around. As souls—as tiny aspects of the Great Mystery, we have a great task before us: instead of marching to the drummer of societal music, we must discover our soul purpose and live inspired by the Divine Feminine and our individual Soul Consciousness. Only then will we live our authentic truth. Only then are we able to make our contribution to society.

A few final thoughts. This book is about *my* soul journey and moves chronologically from childhood forward. It was never meant to be a complete life story, covering all aspects of my life. I always intended to protect the privacy of those who shared their lives with me, especially my former husband, my children, and close and intimate friends. You will find stories about them in every chapter, but the emphasis is on my spiritual journey.

This book is divided into three parts. Part 1 is the narrative of my spiritual journey. For easy and quick reference, many of the spiritual and metaphysical concepts I have worked with throughout my journey are highlighted in part 2 of the book, Metaphysics 101 for the Knowing Woman. In the glossary at the end of the book, you will find brief explanations of the main people, concepts, and places that informed my journey—again, for easy and quick reference. These materials are far from complete; they only touch the surface of a vast body of knowledge available to the seeker. My hope is to whet your appetite, to encourage you to set out on your own soul journey. To assist you on that journey, in part 3 of the book (Workbook for the Soul), I have included questions that can be used for personal reflection or group discussions.

Finally, as a shamanic astrologer, I read the charts of events and individuals for in-depth understanding. As I look back on my life, figuring out the planetary influences that helped or hindered me on my journey has been an exciting and rewarding adventure, which I share with you throughout the pages of this book. I believe you will find them helpful, and they will perhaps open a new area for you to explore.

PART ONE

My Life as a Knowing Woman

A Woman in My Future

o o o o o o o o o o o o o o o o o o o o o o o o o o o o o o o o o o o o o o o o
"The feminine soul image of a woman is still in great distress
because it has remained in the unconscious …[I]t desperately
needs to be brought … into the consciousness of every day …
[to] be acknowledged and accepted."

—*Irene Claremont de Castillejo, Knowing Woman,*
A Feminine Psychology

In August 1982, when my youngest child, Greg, went to college and my
husband, Stan, retired, he and I moved to California from Washington so
that I could join Ananda, a Hindu-Christian spiritual community. Four
years after I joined the community, I became Assistant Minister at Ananda's
San Francisco center. Later that fall, I went on a pilgrimage to India. With
a group of fifty devotees, I visited sites that Paramahansa Yogananda, our
principle spiritual teacher, had visited decades before.

For months before our departure from San Francisco in November 1986,
my friend Georgia, who lived at the San Francisco center, had researched
Akashic astrologers, asking anyone who had been to India whom they would
recommend. One of the most favorable recommendations was for a man
in Benares, the ancient city of Varanasi. Situated on the banks of the holy
Ganges River, Benares had grown over the centuries into one of the major
cities of India, teaming with three million people.

One day, during that pilgrimage to India, I was returning to our Benares
hotel from carpet shopping when I met up with my friends Georgia and
Beth, who were just climbing into a cab. "Where are you going?" I asked.

"To find an Akashic astrologer someone told me about," Georgia said. "I
have an address and I think I can find him. Come with us."

Akashic Astrology

A form of astrology based on the belief that the positions of heavenly bodies at the time of an individual's birth reflect the person's past, present, and future lives. Akashic astrologers, rare and difficult to find, are said to read the annals of time. From the storehouse of records of everyone who ever lived or will live, they are able to discern one's destiny. Belief in reincarnation, the assumption of the continuity of a soul from lifetime to lifetime, underlies this system of thought.

"Okay," I said and, in the spur of the moment, I jumped in the back seat with them, ready for adventure.

The chance to meet with a real seer in a foreign land was irresistible. Swami Kriyananda, a disciple of Yogananda and founder of the Ananda community where I lived, often told devotees that he had received an exceptionally accurate Akashic reading years before from an Indian astrologer. An Akashic astrologer might tell me who I had been in previous lives, perhaps confirm I had helped to guide explorers into the American Pacific Northwest in the early nineteenth century, as I had intuited from childhood. Maybe I would learn about a life in the sixteenth century in Mongolia. Or, perhaps, he would tell me something more exotic than anything I had ever dreamed. Surely, he could tell me what I should expect as a spiritual devotee in this lifetime. He also might tell me about future lives—although this one seemed full of change and challenge, enough to hold my interest. At the very least, as an astrologer, I hoped to add to my knowledge of the science of the stars.

A mile or two from the hotel, our car joined a colorful melee of bicycles, cows, pedestrians, busses, trucks, and rickshaws. Explaining that a rare, full moon eclipse was developing overhead, our driver inched the car forward through the massing crowd. We wanted to get out and walk, but the driver urged patience, begging us not to leave the vehicle. In India, in 1986, it was highly unusual for women to travel unescorted. A half-million Indians were converging on the banks of the holy Ganges River.

Soon, the broad main street, four lanes wide, became so congested that our taxi could not move. When we came to a complete standstill, our driver said he would wait for us. We continued on foot, threading our way along cobblestone paths between centuries old, crumbling stone buildings.

Quickly, darkness enveloped the narrow street. Numerous bystanders offered to show us the way, but we were cautious. Georgia, who traveled frequently in foreign countries, warned us not to trust anyone. We declined help until we were hopelessly lost.

Finally, we stopped at an intersection to decide what to do. Should we go forward? Return to the cab, assuming we could find our way back? Risk hiring a guide who could lead us anywhere? Many people gathered around, watching the strange, obviously foreign women lost in a dubious part of the city. Soft light filtered through windows and open doors, casting shadows on the curious crowd.

Reluctantly, we engaged the most fluent English speaker from among them, a white-clad man in his late forties. Carrying a kerosene lantern to light the way, he led us a quarter of a mile farther through a maze of winding streets to an astrologer's home.

We met the astrologer—a tall, thin man with graying hair—in his simple, unfurnished dwelling lighted by a single low-wattage bulb. Georgia queried him at length and decided not to have a reading; she was sure he was not the astrologer we had set out to find. She would search for other Akashic astrologers as our tour progressed. Beth, on the other hand, wanted to have her chart read. Since I had been reading astrological charts for years, I felt sure I would be able to tell if he was a legitimate astrologer. Beth and the astrologer agreed on a price, and I listened as he read her chart. Impressed with what he told her, I asked him to read for me.

Squatting on his heels, the astrologer consulted worn texts and made notations on a yellowed scrap of paper for several minutes. Turning to where I sat cross-legged on the floor, he told me in a Bengalese accent that Madame was blessed, wealthy, and had five children. My husband had died. He was more or less accurate: as a renunciate of a spiritual community, I was actually quite poor; in India, since I was able to travel there, I was considered wealthy. I had had five pregnancies—four living children plus a miscarriage. My husband and I were divorced.

Then he made an astounding comment that moved me deeply. "Madame," he said, slowly drawing his words out, "you have very good spiritual karma. In this lifetime, you will be enlightened, and you will help very many people."

He spoke for several minutes before reaching out and tugging the lobe of my right ear. "Madame," he said in a soft whisper, "there is a woman in your future."

I appreciated what he said; parts of it I could confirm, other parts filled me with joy. Still other things he said entirely baffled me. I paid him for the consultation, and Beth and I joined Georgia and our guide outside in the alley to return to the waiting cab. Soon we were back at our hotel with the tour group.

ॐ

Days, weeks, months, and eventually years passed as I pondered the Indian astrologer's curious prediction. For nearly fifty years, since I was eight years old and first heard the voice in my mind, I had believed I had a life mission to help millions of people. How had the astrologer known?

He had told me I would be enlightened and that I would help "very many" people. Five years before, enlightenment—union with the ineffable holy mystery—had compelled me to cut off my entire former life and join Ananda Spiritual Community. Had the astrologer simply spotted the marks of a wannabe saint on a pilgrimage to India and made the most of the opportunity?

On the other hand, despite my interest in spiritual astrology, Beth, Georgia, and I had been completely unaware of the impending full moon eclipse when we sought out the astrologer. In shamanic astrology, which I now practice, the full moon is an auspicious time when old habits brought forward from previous lifetimes can be overshadowed; it is a purification time, an opportunity for the new life intent to break forth. Spirit seemed to have brought about the meeting with the seer.

Most mysterious was the astrologer's prophecy that a woman would enter my life. I am not gay, as the prediction might have implied; nor did I foresee the visit of the Goddess Kali in my morning meditation six months later and the personal devastation that followed. It did not occur to me that the astrologer foretold the emergence of my deeply suppressed, true feminine self—my soul.

Kali, Goddess of Death and Destruction

The Indian Goddess, Kali, known for her fierce appearance, is often shown wearing a necklace of skulls and dancing on the body of her consort, the high god Shiva. Considered one of the most powerful of the feminine goddesses, Kali aids the devotee in spiritual discrimination. Cutting through all obstacles, the fearsome Divine Mother removes all impediments to spiritual enlightenment. Often associated with Lord Shiva, she is arguably the most powerful and important feminine energy in the Hindu pantheon.

Child of the Church

BIRTH TO SIX (1932–1938)
THE CHURCH

I was to have been a boy named George—one could say that even in the womb I was determined to be different.

Warmly welcomed as the daughter of Mary Kies Mills and Marion Julian Pierre Mills, both first-born themselves, a new name was quickly found and within a few days after my birth on November 10, 1932, I was christened at a Catholic Church in southeast Portland, Oregon. My godparents were LeRoy Mills, my father's youngest brother, and Elvira Kies, my mother's second sister. I was baptized Georgianna Faye Mills—Faye after my grandfather, Fay Mills, and Georgianna because Mother admired the name of a prominent Portland woman.

Because I was due on election day, Mother had feared she might not be able to vote for the first time before I was born. Happily, on November 9, the day before I came into the world, she proudly cast her vote for Franklin Delano Roosevelt. That day, the moon and the pioneering planet, Uranus, were together in the sign of Aries. For the country, the date was auspicious, signaling the beginning of the New Deal, recovery from the Great Depression, and vast social reconstruction. For me, it signaled a pioneering life and determined effort to be a conscious, free woman.

As I grew, I came to admire the combination name of George and Anna, masculine and feminine, dragon slayer and grandmother of Jesus. Georgianna helped to define my lifelong drive toward conscious equality. My grandfather Fay provided the inspiration for independent inquiry.

What do people say when they pray? Do they whisper in their minds?

My earliest memories include a solemn man wearing a long, white cassock. My family—my mother, father, two younger brothers, and I—were attending Catholic Mass at St. Edward's Church in North Plains, Oregon.

It was the summer of 1938. I was five and would start school that September. We had just moved from the wicked city to a two-bedroom house on a half-acre of land in Bethany, a few miles west of Portland, Oregon.

I was too young to know that the transformational planet, Pluto, would move that summer from the sign of Cancer into the sign of Leo, too young to know that an age of unbridled power was about to erupt upon an unsuspecting globe. Eighteen months before, Franklin Delano Roosevelt had been elected to a second term as president of the United States. In America, the hidden seeds of economic recovery were sprouting; the Great Depression was loosening its grip on the country. And marvelously, my father was employed full time a few miles away as a laborer at the Portland Gas Company, in the production plant under the Saint John's Bridge on the south side of the Willamette River.

St. Edward's Catholic Church is situated in a small farming community in rural western Oregon. My parents had grown up nearby, both family homes equidistant from the church. My mother and father to be, Mary Kies and Pierre Mills, had met at the church when Dad was twelve and Mother six, and eventually they married there in November 1931.

Mother's natal Sun was located in the sign of Aries; thanks to her determination and persistence, every Sunday we arrived early at the church so that we could sit in the right, front pew with an unobstructed view of the altar. There, under the eyes of the entire congregation, I learned to behave properly—to sit up straight and be quiet, and never turn around to see if my cousins, Mary Lou, Pat, and Jerry, had arrived.

After an interminable wait, the priest, a solemn man wearing a long, white cassock covered by a gold-embroidered garment, entered the church through a door on the left of the altar. Everyone stood. The man made the sign of the cross over us. Then, turning his back on us, he faced the altar and talked to God in words I did not understand.

My father, a tall man with prematurely graying hair, told me the priest spoke in Latin, a language I thought had been used when Jesus lived, a long time before. "*Mea culpa, mea culpa, mea maxima culpa,*" (through my fault, through my fault, through my most grievous fault), the priest thumped his chest, apologizing for everyone's sins. I did not know what sins I had committed, but I imagined I had done something awful. Otherwise, why would he pray for me?

Since I couldn't understand what the priest mumbled, I watched carefully, catching glimpses of black shoes, socks, and trousers under the hem of his cassock. About the time I became so bored that I thought I could not sit still another moment, the priest held up a flat, white biscuit and exclaimed in a voice that made me pay attention, "Through him, with him, and in him, in the unity of the Holy Ghost, all glory and honor is yours, Almighty Father, forever and ever!"

"Amen!" the kneeling people responded. Then, standing up, we recited the Our Father. After that, bigger boys and girls, mothers and fathers, and grandpas and grandmas formed lines and moved to the front of the church. Kneeling at the railing separating the people from the holy altar, they bowed their heads and waited.

Carrying a gold plate piled high with the little, white biscuits, the priest slowly moved from right to left across the church, in front of the row of kneeling people. As each person stuck out his or her tongue, the priest put a white round on it and murmured, "*Corpus Christi*" (Body of Christ). *Why can't I go to the railing? How does it taste?* Fascinated, I watched the men and women, heads bent so low their chins touched their chests, return to their seats to kneel with hands folded and eyes closed to pray.

After Mass every Sunday, I loved to run outside to find Grandpa Mills. He dropped Grandma off every Sunday, drove to Maize's General Store a half mile away in North Plains to buy a newspaper, and returned to the churchyard to read it. As a boy, he had attended the Presbyterian Church, but when he married Grandma, he had promised their children would be raised Catholic. In the church that I grew up in, one had to be baptized Catholic to go to heaven when one died. The alternative was hell. Long before I was old enough to remember, Grandma taught my cousins and me to pray that Grandpa would become a Catholic. All the family prayed for him.

Every Sunday, we had dinner at one of my grandparents' homes. The best visits were at the Mills' farm where, after we had eaten dessert, everyone sat around the round oak table and talked. My father and his younger brothers, Fritz and Leroy, crossed their legs and tilted their carved oak chairs back so far I thought they might fall—and secretly hoped they would!

My grandfather rested his crippled right arm, injured in a sawmill accident years before, on his knee. Pulling a Bull Durham sack from his shirt pocket, he spread tobacco on a small paper on the table, rolled the paper up, and placed the cigarette in the corner of his mouth. Holding a matchbox in his lame hand, Grandpa struck a stick match against the side of the box with his good left hand. When the match flamed, he lit the cigarette clamped between his lips, dropped the match in an ashtray, took a long drag, and removed the cigarette from his mouth. Turning to my father, his oldest son, born under the sign of Leo, he asked, "Well, Pierre, what did the priest say?"

Since Grandpa Mills was deaf, everyone spoke loudly, gesturing to emphasize words and meanings. Their voices started low, increased in pitch and volume as the argument intensified until sound bounced off the kitchen ceiling. "How can he say that?" "Well, there might be some truth in it ..." "What do you mean? Why, in the Catholic paper last week, the pope said ..." "Ah, hell, you don't have to listen to him. What does he know? Let him talk about faith and morals. How we free Americans vote is our business." The last statement came from my independent, articulate father.

The Sunday discussions appealed to my natural sense of independence and self-actualization. The more the grownups shouted, the more I liked it. Listening to them, I learned that freedom and personal responsibility were more important than what the pope, an old man in a long dress and a pointed gold hat, who lived in a palace on the other side of the world, said—even if he was the head of the Holy Roman Catholic Church.

Longing for Love

When I was five years old, our neighbors who lived in the brick house across the lane from our little cottage invited me one day to play with Carolyn, their visitor, a girl a year or two older than me. I felt very important to be invited; they did not have children, but they had a real sandbox in their backyard. Solid two-by-fours, nailed to corner posts and set in the ground, formed the edges of the box that held six inches of real sand. My new friend and I kicked off our shoes and climbed into the sandbox. Busily, we sifted sand into cone-shaped piles, built mountains and valleys, and filled shiny metal buckets using little, red-handled shovels.

Carolyn sipped a bottle of orange pop, a luxury my family could not afford. When the glass bottle was empty, she casually dropped it beside her.

"Don't leave that," I scolded. "It might break. Someone could get hurt."

Carolyn shrugged and went on playing. Sure enough, it broke, for when I stood up a few minutes later, I stepped on a broken piece: I reached for the small rake at the edge of the box, sand squished through my toes, and I felt a slicing sensation. Blood spurted from my right big toe, and a rusty red clump of sand quickly formed in front of my foot. I tried to wiggle my toe, but it would not move.

In a panic, I crossed the gravel road to our house and sobbed out my story. Mother must have wrapped my foot in a clean towel and applied pressure to stop the bleeding; she must have called my father from the garage where he was working; she must have phoned the doctor at his home. I remember only the half-hour trip to Portland. It seemed an eternity.

Dad drove our Model A Ford. On his right, in the passenger seat, Mother held sturdy, two-year-old Louis. Freckle-faced, four-year-old Norm, faded bib overalls hanging on his thin body, perched next to me on the back seat, his dark eyes solemn under a light brown cowlick. With my feet on the transmission hump, I sat in the middle of the seat and leaned forward, inserting my body in the space between the front seats. Squeezing as close to my parents as I could manage, I watched my father negotiate the hairpin turns of the narrow, macadam-paved Old Germantown road.

After parking across from the city park, close to the entrance of a tall, brick building, my father picked me up and carried me into the marble-faced lobby. Mother trailed behind with Norman and Louis. Dad pushed a button on the wall, and when the iron lattice gate in front of us opened, we entered a creaky elevator and rode up to the fourth floor where Dr. Wayne Stratford, our family doctor, waited in the hallway. He pointed the way to the examining room; my father carried me in and sat me down on a paper-covered table.

Dr. Stratford examined my foot briefly, then turned to my parents and said, "I'll give her gas to put her to sleep."

Gas? I trembled.

I had heard my father, who worked at the Gas Company, once tell my mother, "It's dangerous work, Mary. I could die if a line broke." Now, my father nodded agreement.

Grandpa Mills puts injured animals to sleep; they never wake up! I searched for an escape. I quickly took in the whole room. The deep, white porcelain sink where the doctor had washed his hands offered no reprieve. Nor did the shelves above the sink where someone had arranged various metal instruments. There was nowhere to go. I had been taught that big girls did not cry; my brothers especially were often spanked for not doing what they were told to do. In my panic, I thought, *If I cry, I'll be spanked.*

The doctor held a large, thick, deflated, red rubber bag. A hose dangling from it connected to a stainless steel box on wheels. He instructed me, "Blow up the balloon."

Repeating the instructions, my father urged, "Blow up the balloon."

Surely, I can trust them, can't I?

"You'll sleep while I sew up your toe," Dr. Stratford said.

Maybe I'll wake up. And maybe I won't.

Stifling a sob, I took a breath and blew.

ॐ

When I woke, strips of adhesive tape and white gauze bandages wrapped my foot from toe to ankle. "The tendon that moves her big toe was cut through. I sewed it together. Don't let her walk for a week," the doctor told my parents. Looking kindly at me, he smiled and said, "If you're lucky, you won't limp."

My father carried me from the office. Behind us, Mother's and the boys' footsteps clattered on the hardwood floors. The sound echoed down the long, empty corridor. At the end of the hallway, I watched as the lift slowly rose on the other side of the latticed metal doors.

Inside the elevator as we began the descent, my father shifted his feet and sighed loudly. "My God, girl," he said, "you're a dead weight."

"What's a dead weight, Daddy?" I asked.

"There's no give to it. You're as heavy as a hundred-pound sack of grain."

I'm too big!

I wanted his arms around me, holding me, stroking my shoulders. I wanted him to say I was his little girl. I wanted to know he was happy I would live. I wanted reassurance that my foot would heal and I would walk like everyone else.

I thought, *I should have moved the bottle. I should have left the sandbox. I've caused too much expense—where will the money for the gas and the doctor come from? I'm too big. Mother is busy with the boys; she doesn't have time for me. How can I make Daddy proud ... Everyone says I'm smart ... If I do well when I go to school, maybe Daddy will love me.*

I did not visit the Nicholson's again. And I never saw Carolyn, not even to say good-bye.

Seven to Eleven (Summer 1940 - Summer 1944)
A Life Mission

The Catholic Church teaches that children reach the age of reason at seven. At that age, a child is able to tell the difference between right and wrong. Conscious in this way, a child baptized at birth reaches a new stage of spiritual growth. She or he can now receive the Sacraments of Reconciliation and Holy Eucharist.

For a renegade thinker, a questioning mind such as my own, the years between seven and eleven opened up vast new territory. I became aware that women were often trapped by their bodies, that men were in charge of the world, and that words and education were a precious escape.

During this period, when my soul voice spoke for the first time, I learned my mission in life: to help millions. Comprehensively under the influence of church, family, and society, my thoughts, if not my actions, began the creative, demanding process of individuation.

Boys Are More Like Jesus, Dear

My classmates and I lined up outside St. Edward's Church on a Sunday in late June. For the previous two weeks, we had prepared for our First Holy Communion in a special catechism class held at a nearby local school. Nuns from St. Mary's of the Valley Convent several miles away stayed with local parishioners during the week; daily, they inculcated the teachings of the church and impressed upon us gawky, farm children the solemnity of what we were about to undertake. I was seven years old and had completed the second grade a few weeks before.

Beside the narrow gravel path where we waited, waxy buttercups and foot-high grasses beginning to go to seed swayed in a light breeze. On this beautiful, early summer day, the sun shone from a cloud-studded blue sky. The lilacs and forsythia had long ago faded; white snowball bushes and tall, blue flowers bloomed. From inside the church, sounds of a foot-pedaled organ drifted.

Sister Mary Francis gave the cue, and the music swelled. We mounted the wooden steps and marched into the building singing, "Faith of our fathers, holy faith, we will be true to thee 'til death," in our off-key piping voices. I remember feeling very proud as I stepped up the aisle between the rows of people; I knew I would always be true to holy faith.

The boys, dressed in white shirts, black pants, and black ties, their unruly hair plastered down with water, led the procession and took seats in the left, front pew. Wearing shimmering gossamer veils, white dresses, white knee socks, and white patent leather shoes, we girls followed, slipping into the row behind the boys as the nuns had instructed.

When the time for Holy Communion arrived, the boys approached the rail first and knelt. Like baby sparrows in the nest, the fledgling men tipped back their heads, their mouths opened wide to receive the Body of Christ.

I had asked during practice, "Why do the boys get to go first?"

"Boys are more like Jesus, dear," Sister Steven Marie had answered in her soft, cool voice.

As I knelt at the communion rail, I smarted with injustice. *I'm bigger and smarter than my brothers. I'm a year older than Norman and two and a half years older than Louis, but they're boys, so when they grow up, they'll get to go first. I'm the oldest ... I take care of them. It's not fair.*

I never had anyone to talk to about these matters. At seven, it did not occur to me to ask my father why the boys went first. My Leo father would have tried to explain. Mother, the Aries general, enforced the rules; I would not have asked her. No child my age was asking the question I had, and neither were most adults. In 1939, the role of women was simply never questioned, particularly not in a Catholic household. Nor can I imagine they would have been questioned in most households, anywhere in the world. The church made the rules; it had been the law from time immemorial.

I would graduate from college with honors, marry, have four children, and become the primary breadwinner for my family before I began to make decisions contrary to what church dogma mandated. Twenty-five years after my First Communion, in my thirties, I would conclude that men could not be the arbiters of my life. In my forties, I would finally see that my childhood inculcation had been so thorough, it had impacted my thought processes. We were taught, under threat of hell and damnation, that even thoughts contrary to church teaching were sinful, and so I trained myself to avoid certain thinking, especially in the sexual context. What eleven-year-old child wants to tell a priest in the confessional that she thought of kissing a boy?

Despite the innovation and pioneering spirit reflected in my astrological chart, I was crushed by the overwhelming weight of cultural and religious expectations. The T-square of Pluto, planet of power and manipulation, and of Saturn, planet of authority and structure, to my Moon/Uranus conjunction in Aries, saw to that. This planetary complex represented the greatest challenge of my life and the greatest opportunity for learning.

Pat's Story

Although I must have heard the story much earlier, my first memory of Grandma Mills telling my cousins, Mary Lou and Pat, and me the story of Pat's birth was when I was seven years old. My nearly six-foot tall grandmother sat at the round kitchen table, the print fabric of her dress covering her broad lap. Pat stood close, within Grandma's circling arm. Smiling, Grandma told her, "You were Flossie's third baby in four years. Before your Ma showed real good, she went out of her mind. Fritz had to take her to Salem, to the asylum for the mentally ill."

The three of us leaned close. "The doctor told Fritz, 'Your wife is too ill to carry this child. I don't see how both of them can live. Who do you want me to save?'

"Fritz asked Father Kilpatrick, who said, 'You must save the child. It hasn't been baptized.' Right then, I started praying."

Mary Lou, a few months older than me, interrupted, her voice tremulous, "The priest said Mom should die?"

"The doctor said it was her or the baby. Flossie had lost a lot of weight and didn't know where she was. The baby—you, Pat—had a slight chance to live.

"Flossie was inside walls, you know. The night before you were born, they moved Flossie to the hospital across the street." She squeezed Pat's hand, "They didn't want your birth certificate to say you were born in an insane asylum. It's a miracle you both lived!" Grandma wiped her eyes with the hem of her apron.

"You were born premature. The doctor said you couldn't survive, so we brought you home to die." She pointed to the gold band on the second finger of her left hand. "You were so tiny you wore my wedding ring as a bracelet."

"I know! I know! You're going to give it to me when you die." Pat stroked the ring. "Tell how you saved my life."

"I toasted bread on the back of that stove." Grandma gestured toward a cast iron woodstove. "After the bread was brown and hard, I soaked it in water. Then I filled an eyedropper with the golden water and fed it to you, a drop at a time. The doctor said you wouldn't live, but you did. You're my miracle baby!"

Again and again, we begged Grandma to tell the tale. It was a miracle story, a survival story about one of us; we loved hearing it. I tried to imagine how tiny Pat's hand must have been to fit inside a gold wedding ring.

Only when I grew older, after I began to menstruate, did it occur to me that when I married and became pregnant, the church would hold my life hostage, too. Childbirth was dangerous; mothers often died. It seemed to me that unbaptized babies were more important than their baptized mothers. A mother would be sacrificed to save her baby, so the child could be baptized and saved for eternity. I might not be as fortunate as Aunt Flossie who had survived the doctor's and the priest's dire predictions. The church could ask me to die. To save my babies, I could die.

I Have To Be Free

In the summer of 1940, when I was not quite eight, I was ironing in the living room of our home on Cornelius Pass Road just outside Portland, Oregon. Sighing, I smoothed a white cotton pillowcase embroidered with hearts and flowers, sprayed water on the four-inch hem edged with crocheted lace, and moved the heavy electric iron back and forth. A cloud of steam rose from the cloth-covered board.

From the box radio on the table at the end of the couch, a man's voice interrupted big band music. Every hour on the hour, I thought, pulling a tiny dress with tatted lace on the collar from the overflowing cardboard box we used as a clothes hamper. Except for the smocking on the bodice, I thought I could iron it well enough to gain Mother's approval.

Glancing around, my gaze rested on an overstuffed couch and chair. I thought, We have more money now. My parents had purchased living room furniture, bunk beds for the boys, and installed shining brown and yellow linoleum in the living room. Daddy goes to work every day.

Mother, who had just checked on Lorry, my sixteen-month-old sister in the playpen out on the front porch, entered the living room.

"Mama," I asked, "what are we going to buy next?"

For a moment, she stood there looking at me, making a decision about how much she thought I would understand or should know. When she spoke, her voice trembled, "We're going to have another baby."

My breath slowed. My heart thumped. I thought of Lorry on the porch. "Another baby?" I said. "We have one."

"Yes," Mother nodded slowly, "in January." I watched her dark, sad eyes. "It's a secret. Don't tell the boys."

My mind raced. *Does my father know? Mother's sisters? Her stomach will get big again. Another baby! I'll never have Mama all to myself. There'll be more work.* My throat hurt and I wanted to cry. I swallowed. Mother always said I should be a big girl.

Mother went into the bedroom, and I continued to iron. *When I grow up, I'll have babies, too. Boys are free. They work outside, but Mother and I stay in the house, cooking and cleaning and doing housework. I want to be free.*

My cousins seem to think having babies is a grand idea. Why they even play with dolls, an entertainment that bores me to tears. My cousins simper about dresses and hairdos and act plain silly. When there's a baby around, they always want to play with it. Not me, all I do is take care of my brothers and my sister. Why would I want to have babies?

I set the iron upright on the heat-stained cloth. Hoping Mother would not catch me, I slipped out through the kitchen. Behind me, the screen door smacked against the jam.

Mother called, "Georgianna, come back! You haven't finished your ironing."

Pretending not to hear, I ran. Maybe she would spank me, but I did not care. I had to be free.

The Power of Words

Whenever I round a particular turn on the curving road we traveled to my grandparents' home when I was a child, I remember asking, "What does that word mean, Daddy?

He explained, using another word I did not know. Reveling in his attention, I asked question after question until he exclaimed, "Oh, for God's sake, go look it up in the dictionary!"

He had never said that before. I was enormously honored that he thought I could, and at the same time, I was afraid that I would fail. What if I could not find the word? I'd never know! Already, at eight years old, knowing was very important to me.

My father talked about fascinating ideas—philosophy, religion, and politics, how things worked and why they were the way they were. He knew so many wonderful words. For me, he provided access to magical kingdoms. He rolled words around in his mouth, each separate syllable uttered in a deep, sonorous tone. Teasing my brothers and me, he said in-du-bit-a-bly when he was certain; he never said canyon if chasm better described a hole in the earth.

On an end table next to Mother's rocking chair in the living room, my parents kept an outsized *Webster's Comprehensive Dictionary*, so large I could hardly lift it. Heavy with the wondrous things my father knew and I could learn, that dictionary held the key to the world of grownups, to great ideas and famous people, to distant lands, to the solar system, even—I imagined— the key to the meaning of life.

In contrast, Mother also kept a large white Bible on the end table. We sometimes looked at the pictures in the book. Bible passages were a part of every Catholic Mass and the priest usually preached on their message. In catechism class, we learned Bible stories, but we never read the Bible, probably because prior to Vatican II, the Catholic Church primarily oriented to ritual and sacraments. As a child, *The Baltimore Catechism*, a book that set out the beliefs of a Catholic in question-and-answer form, to be memorized, was far more important.

Many years later, I would express surprise to my pastor that the church had never emphasized reading the Bible, while my non-Catholic neighbors read it as a principal means of practicing their faith. He responded that generally lay people had not read the Bible because it was written in a language not well understood by modern Catholics.

Pioneers and Indians

As my siblings and I grew, Dad told us marvelous family stories intimately bound to the rivers, mountains, and pioneer-cleared valleys of the Oregon Territory. Although I very recently learned that many of my father's tales were historically and genealogically inaccurate, it is a fact that my European ancestors first arrived in the Oregon Territory in the late 1840's by wagon train. Angelique Marcellais Gagnon, my great, great, great, grandmother, a Metis Indian, and Francois Xavier Gagnon, my great, great, great, grandfather, traveled with their five children in the Sinclair Party that crossed the Rockies by wagon train. Their granddaughter, my great grandmother, Mary Louisa Dupuis, was baptized at Fort Vancouver where Archbishop Blanchet (a distant relation) and Dr. John McLaughlin had lived. Her grandfather, Louis Dupuis (my great great great great grandfather) was one of the first French fur traders in the Oregon Territory in the 1830's. The baptismal register at the Catholic Church in Vancouver includes the names of Rosella Marie Burgy, my grandmother, in the mid-1880s, and Marion Julian Pierre Mills, my father, in 1905.

In 1888, five years after President Ulysses S. Grant drove the Golden Spike completing the Northern Pacific transcontinental railroad, Fay Mills, the six-year-old destined to become my grandpa, traveled from South Dakota to the Washington Territory.

I loved my father's stories of our pioneering relatives, and I grieved with him, tears slowly running down his cheeks, as he described the defeat of Nez Perce Indian Chief Joseph in the snows of Idaho. I grew up believing I was related to Chief Joseph, and I taught my grandchildren the story of his brave leadership, how he led a tiny band of Indians toward Canada, and almost made it there. Caught just forty miles south of the border, many of the men of the tribe killed, the children and women emaciated and starving, Chief Joseph had declared, "From this day forward, I will fight no more."

Captured by the United States Army, he had been taken east as a showpiece before being returned to Washington State. Never permitted to return to his homeland in Oregon's Wallowa Mountains, he lived the rest of his life in captivity on the Colville Indian Reservation north of Spokane.

Charmed by the story of Chief Joseph and my ancestry of brave women and men of both Indian and European extraction, I knew that I must defend the precious freedom achieved and lost at such great personal cost. Of course, Indian spirituality was never a part of my early awareness; in later life, it would become an important aspect of my spirituality.

Politics, in my family, was a respected profession. Andrew Jackson Mills, my great-grandfather, served as a sergeant-at-arms in the first Washington State legislature. In 1891, he was elected state representative; two decades later, his oldest son, my great-uncle Chapin, represented the district as state senator. In my family home, politics were boisterously debated, and I took an early interest in political issues. Because I was a girl, I knew that I could never be involved in politics as the men in my family had been. And then I discovered my life mission.

A Life Mission

Before school recessed for the summer of 1941, my third-grade teacher, Mrs. Trachsel, sent me to the principal's office. She seemed pleased, but I was quite frightened. I could not imagine what I had done wrong. Waiting on a straight-back chair under the watchful eye of the school secretary, I squirmed and worried about what was to become of me.

Eventually, the smiling principal invited me into his office. He seemed awfully pleased and he wanted me to relax, but I was very puzzled; I didn't know what was coming. The God-like man seated me on a chair facing a desk as wide as the Pacific Ocean and took his seat on the opposite side. "Your parents and I," he told me, "have decided you will start fifth grade next fall. Mrs. Trachsel will give you books to study over the summer."

I get to read fourth grade books! I thought. *But … what if I can't keep up? He says I can go back to my class if the studies are too hard, but the kids would make fun of me, and my parents would be very disappointed. Oh, well. I have to try; maybe it will turn out all right.*

The following Sunday, while we were visiting Mother's parents, my father called Norman, Louis, and me into the living room. Angry over some mischief one of us had gotten into, he yelled, "Were you all behind a door when the brains were passed out?"

I looked down at the mysterious, several-inch wide, white conch shell that had held open the door between the kitchen and living room for as long as I could remember. I had asked where the shell with the undulant curves and luminescent pink interior came from. No one knew. Perhaps, I sometimes daydreamed, it had washed up on the shore of a distant island where warm, gentle waves rolled upon the shore, palm trees swayed, and melodious music played—a place where everyone was loved, a place where no one yelled. A place that was not conflicted like my life was.

I thought smugly, *I wasn't behind that door—I'm too smart. My dad says so; my teacher and the principal say so.*

As quickly as the thought formed, a mature woman's voice spoke in my mind. Emphatically, it said, *You are gifted—but not for yourself. In your lifetime, you must help millions of people.*

So authoritative was the voice that my self-identity instantly reorganized. Years would pass before I heard the voice again, yet the message was clear and unequivocal. I had no doubt. I knew my life purpose. And I could not share it with anyone. People would think that if I heard voices, something was wrong with me.

How I would help others was a mystery, but from then on, all my decisions were measured against the mandate the voice had given. To help millions became the unspoken focus of my life.

Over the years, I often wondered about the message. It was pompous and exaggerated. How would I help millions?

Now, as a shamanic astrologer, I know that Venus, the planet that describes a person's feminine quality, returns to its natal position every eight years. When I first heard the voice, Venus had just begun her new cycle as a morning star. It is striking that my soul self made the announcement of a life mission at just that time.

Summer Catechism

Every summer, for two weeks, the Sisters of the Holy Name—austere women in long, black habits—taught catechism classes in a vacant public school a block from St. Edward's Church. In my second-year class, Sister Mary Joseph described countless souls in purgatory who could not save themselves. Poised on the brink between heaven and hell, depending on our prayerful appeals, they would either fall into a blazing abyss or rise up to heaven to join angels surrounding Almighty God on his golden throne.

I reasoned that there were so many in purgatory that some souls must be poised on the brink of redemption, closer to release than others. I schemed about how I could help the greatest number escape their endless torment.

After Sister Mary Joseph agreed that even the smallest prayer would release a soul from purgatory, I began to pray for those needing the least help. That way, I calculated, more souls would escape from the flames to join the heavenly chorus. "Jesus, Mary, Joseph, there goes another one," I counted before falling asleep every night. During the day, whenever I thought of it, I would repeat the prayer. Truth be told, I believed the souls I helped into heaven would in turn save me. I wasn't saintly; I bargained for my own safe arrival in heaven.

The nuns who taught us moved quietly and sedately, always two by two. They were God's servants, humble vessels of the peace that passeth understanding. Sworn to chastity for life, these Brides of Christ belonged to God. I feared and admired their separation from the ordinary world—their lives of prayer, nursing, and teaching; yet, they seemed ethereal, not quite real.

In contrast, priests—even pink-cheeked, young men fresh out of the seminary—were arbiters of virtue and morality. They gave up sex, marriage, and parenthood to become Jesus in the world. Inseparable from the Catholic Church that had begun nearly two thousand years before, priests—sometimes wearing red, square hats and gowns with six-inch lace hems—made the rules. They decided what was right and what was wrong. When priests spoke, God spoke; when they absolved my sins, God forgave me.

A priest's competence to interpret the Holy Word or even to absolve sins paled to insignificance when compared to his miraculous capacity to turn ordinary bread and wine into the Body and Blood of Jesus Christ. This was a key tenet of the church. When the priest said the words over the bread and wine, they became actual flesh and blood. This was not ritual or pretense; this was real. Through a mystery beyond comprehension, consecrated wafers of unleavened flour and fermented grape juice became flesh and blood, the living body of Jesus Christ reincarnated before us. On this crucial point of faith, the pulsing heart of Catholicism, hinged my status as a true believer— and any possibility of personal salvation.

Only priests could touch the Holy of Holies. Only priests could offer the Divine Sacrifice to God the Father. What is more, only men, then and still today, could be priests—never women.

At eight years of age, I knew that, in the eyes of the Catholic Church, women were inferior to men. This attitude of superiority of men on the part of church and society shaped every aspect of my and every other woman's life, defining what we could and could not do in intimate relations and in social settings. Life itself was a vast game of politics to be lived as a compromise: do what you can as an independent person, pretend when necessary, and conform to be loved and accepted.

Rescuing a Snake

That summer of 1941 before the Second World War began, my brother Norman and I attended band practice in the basement of our country school one night a week. One evening, after early dismissal, some thirty-five or forty of us—second graders to big kids in the eighth grade—waited for our rides. Whiling away the time, a third-grade boy caught a garden snake and waved it around. With shrieks, the girls scattered; the older boys grinned and cheered him on, "Hey, Darrell, way to go!"

Angry with the boy, I (Joan of Arc, Savior of Abused Snakes) came to the rescue. I chased Darrell, straining fast up the cut of the hill where he darted above the parking lot. When I caught his shirt, he shoved the snake toward me. I felt the awful scaly skin on the palm of my hand. My stomach heaved and my hand trembled as I grabbed the snake from his hand and flung it over the fence. The writhing reptile undulated twenty feet through the air, landing in a cow pasture.

As quickly as I had pitied the snake, I felt sorry for the defeated boy. I leaned over and kissed him. The schoolyard exploded with laughter.

Oh, shame upon shame!

Letting go of the boy's arm, I ran down the incline. Shocked that I had held the snake—proper young women shied away from creepy crawly creatures—the girls turned away. Awed—stunned may be the better word—that a mere girl had performed so well, the boys shuffled from one foot to the other, taking a new-found interest in the black macadam surface of the playground. In the silence, their thoughts spoke deafeningly. I had broken the rules—handled a snake—bested a boy, and kissed him!

Inadvertently, I had broken the rules. I felt terrible. Once again, I had stepped outside the norm of good girl behavior, and I did not fit in. My sense of justice and my quick action had made me the laughing stock of the school.

Recalling this incident years later, I would view my defense of the snake as a harbinger of events to come. The Christian myth of Eve tempted by the devil in the form of a serpent and the Hindu belief that snakes represent the Divine Feminine are literally and figuratively continents apart. One negates a woman; the other elevates her to divine status. It had taken fifty years for me to embrace the Divine Feminine. At eight, I simply defended her right to life.

I Wonder If George Washington

I had begun fifth grade in the fall of 1941, eager to please my parents by succeeding with my studies and anxious to fit in with my classmates, all a year or two older than me. Ridiculed for being smart, taller than most of the girls and all of the boys, looking for and finding no friends, I struggled through the first several months.

At school, one afternoon after class dismissal, LaVonne, a sixth grader, looked carefully around the empty classroom before furtively pulling a writing book from her desk and thumbing the pages. Pointing to where someone had written –u-c-k after the capital letter F, she looked up expectantly. Seeing that I was puzzled about the word, she twittered, "Don't you know?"

"Know what?"

"Oh, I can't tell," she stammered, hugging her waist.

While she would not tell me what the word meant or about sexuality in general, she did not hesitate to tell our classmates that I did not know. When they laughed, I began to think the word held the key to the successful completion of my entire life. When I could not find it in our home dictionary, or in the huge book at school, I asked my younger brothers if they knew what the word meant. They were as innocent as me.

I asked Bobby Gunderson, our neighbor in the fourth grade. He said he knew what the word meant, but he was too embarrassed to tell me. I was taller and heavier than Bobby, so after begging him repeatedly to tell me, when he still would not, I tackled him and took him down. Straddling him on the muddy, cold ground at the edge of the bog where our summer garden grew, I demanded, "Tell me, or I won't let you up."

"No, no. I can't."

"Why?"

"Can't tell a girl."

"Tell me."

Finally, he capitulated. His clumsy explanation lacked anatomical details, but it seemed logical. I accepted it as a matter of fact. Mother had given me a book to read about menstruation that had a little information about intercourse. And of course from church, I knew that boys and girls did not "do it."

A week later, angry with my brother Norman, proud of my new information, and thinking I was out of range of Mother's keen ear, I yelled, "F--- you."

"Where did you learn that filth?" Mother shrieked. "You'll go to hell."

Now, not only my social and scholastic future, but also the fate of my soul hung in the balance. I was the butt of the joke at school, and no one was going to tell me anything more. And here my mother was announcing that I was going to hell. My soul would be lost forever.

"One of the girls at school showed it to me in a book. She wouldn't tell me what it meant."

"Who told you what it meant?"

"I made Bobby tell. It's not his fault."

She spanked me with the wooden paddle she kept in a kitchen drawer, washed my mouth out with soap, and forbade my brothers and me to play with our friends for a month.

I had not been paddled since I started school. It hurt physically; my buttocks stung where the wooden paddle had hit. I would not be using the word again, but the deepest damage was to my psyche. The tears I shed were from emotional hurt. For several years, I had thought that I was a grown-up Mother's helper. I was too old to be treated so poorly. Obviously, she had no respect for me; I was only someone to boss around. I had longed for the time when she would finally give me the love I had never received. Now I knew I would never have it. Always there was another child to be cared for. She did not trust me. I was only a pawn in her world. I decided to never again tell her anything. This was a large, important decision. I was not ready to act independently, but my thoughts were going in that direction.

In February, when Miss Smith assigned writing projects to celebrate the presidents' birthdays, I wrote about George Washington, the Father of Our Country, who admitted he had cut down a cherry tree. *My truthfulness cost me my only friends. Why did truth work for him, but not for me?* I wrote:

> *I wonder if George Washington*
> *When he was nine years old—*
> *Turned up his toes*
> *And combed his hair,*
> *And did as he was told?*
> *I wonder if he never said,*
> *"Oh dear!"*
> *When he was sent to bed?*

In the face of parental authority, "Oh, dear" was a gigantic self-assertion, a flying in the face of all that was good and proper. True to the strong connection of Uranus and the moon in Aries in my natal astrological chart, I struggled to write that I was an individual with ideas different from my parents and teachers, at the same time knowing I could not, must not, risk their anger. I worked very hard on my poem, changing it repeatedly.

Miss Smith gave me an "A" and asked me to read the poem before the fifth and sixth grades. Certain my classmates hated me for being the youngest and smartest kid in the class, knees shaking and voice trembling, I read the poem.

A front-row boy sneered. "Turned up his toes—what does that mean?"

Partly rhyme and partly rhythm, I thought it said George Washington looked smart, respectful, and alert.

A fifth-grade toughie scoffed to the room at large, "She didn't write that."

"Who did you copy?" bantered a frizzy-haired sixth-grade girl.

My magical poem—my valiant self-assertion—had been muddied, tossed away by cruel young minds. I was a plagiarist, someone who stole other people's ideas; I felt their awful scorn.

I was very sad. I was trying so hard to make my parents proud. I really wanted to succeed in the fifth grade, and I wanted to have friends. Yet, no matter what I did, the other kids laughed at me. I was always too big, or too young, or too smart. They always found something to tease me about. I had been totally engaged in writing the poem, expressing a sense of injustice in a way that I thought would be respectful and true. My mother had abandoned me, I thought. There was no help there. I could not give up. What could I do but soldier on?

Weeks later, measles swept through the school. Absences of more than three days required a doctor's signature before a student could return to class. Unless we were seriously ill, my brothers and I never stayed home more than two days. When a few spots appeared under my arms, I did not tell Mother, forestalling her certain instruction, "You're not sick; go to school."

One day after I had the measles, Miss Smith asked me to work a problem on the blackboard. When I could not see what she had written, she moved me from my seat in the back of the class to a desk in the middle of the room. When I still could not see the writing, I joined the rowdiest boys in the front row. Mortified to be there, I did not want my mother and father to know, but, to my chagrin, the teacher sent a note home.

The examination at an optometrist shop in downtown Portland confirmed that the measles, as innocuous as they had seemed, had ruined my eyesight. My parents ordered little, round, gold-rimmed glasses for me—the kind simpering old maids wore.

Ridiculed for my sexual innocence and my intellectual ability, and wearing spinster glasses that I passionately hated, I withdrew. Kids did not wear glasses then, or so I recall. I was afraid that the glasses emphasized my scholarly bent and separated me from most children my age. I went into hiding. Books became my companions. Except for rare and greatly welcomed visits with my cousins, Mary Lou and Pat, I had no girl friends. During the two years that I attended sixth and seventh grades, my playmates were younger boys, our neighbors next door, and my brothers. Every night, I talked myself to sleep, making up stories, whispering dialogue for hours between clever friends and myself, directing happy adventures. In my imagination, I was the heroine; people turned to me for guidance, welcomed my interventions, and loved me unconditionally. I would not be as despondent again until reprimanded for a bad attitude at Ananda nearly fifty years later.

TWELVE TO NINETEEN (1945 - SUMMER 1952) TEEN YEARS

Remember Who You Are!

Life began to make sense again after my parents purchased acreage and we moved to a logging community on the Nehalem River in Oregon's Pacific Coast Range. There, in September 1944, my brothers and I joined other students in a two-room schoolhouse. John Berg, Delmar Jepson, George Bellingham, and I composed the entire eighth grade.

In my teen years, my cousins, Mary Lou and Pat, and I lived on our grandparents' farm in the summers. Earning money to buy our clothing and incidentals during the school year, we picked strawberries, hoed and fertilized vines, harvested green beans and broccoli, and hired out at neighboring farms. Best of all, I was with my cousins.

One evening during the first summer, Grandpa, Grandma, my cousins, and I sat talking after dinner at the old oak table. Anticipating that my hard-of-hearing, non-Catholic grandfather could be enticed into saying something scandalous, I grinned at my cousins and asked, "How did God make us, Grandpa?"

Gesturing to show the shaping of a human figure, he boomed, "I cannot understand how anyone, even God himself, can take a piece of clay, shape it with two arms, two legs, and a head, blow on it, and poof, it's a man."

We laughed. Grandma leaned close to me and whispered, "You don't want to pay attention. Mr. Mills is a good man—but he's not Catholic, you know." Like other women born in the late nineteenth century, Grandma usually referred to my grandfather as Mister in public.

When they married, Grandpa had agreed to raise their children Catholic, but he refused to acknowledge her Indian ancestry. We all knew that Grandma was one-eighth Indian, but that information was too inflammatory for the Republican Presbyterian culture Grandpa had grown up in; Grandpa had denied her Indian heritage when they were courting and continued to do so for his entire life.

Grandma had taught my father to be proud of his background, and from as early as I recall, my father proudly enumerated the eight bloodlines we carried—Scotch, Irish, English, German, French, Luxembourgian, Dutch, and the very special American Indian. He never let us forget that we were products of the American melting pot.

Grandma never mentioned her Indian heritage in Grandpa's presence, yet she made sure we all knew. One evening, she and I were cutting roses from her prize garden west of the house. Scissors in one hand, a long-stemmed American Beauty in the other, her tall figure limned in the light of the setting sun, she gestured toward an outbuilding and said, "When your father was nine, I took him over there and told him my grandmother Julienne was half Indian. Your father is named after her, you know."

Still pointing, she shook her finger and told me, "Don't forget! Remember who you are!"

I can't recall what she told me at the time about my great-great-great grandmother, Julienne Modeste Demers Dupuis. Recently, I learned she had borne twenty-two children, eleven of whom lived to adulthood. One of them was Nicolas Joseph Dupuis, father of my grandmother Rosella. I've visited the graves of Julienne and three of her children who died in childhood on a single day. I can't imagine the sadness my great-great-great grandmother endured, and I am grateful to the brave women who birthed a line of strong women.

Taking Matters Into Their Own Hands

Coming upon a faded photo one evening, I recalled the story my grandparents often told of how Grandpa Mills stopped attending the Catholic Church. Grandpa would begin, telling how he had joined the Knights of Pythias, one of many Masonic organizations then flourishing throughout the United States, before Grandpa and Grandma married. He would describe in detail how, after they purchased their farm near North Plains in 1905, he and Grandma helped organize local chapters of the Knights and its counterpart, the Pythian Sisters. They helped build the Masonic Hall in North Plains and had been socializing with friends there for more than a decade before, in the late 1920s, the Pope forbade Catholics to be Masons. Anyone who disobeyed would be expelled from the church.

Following papal direction, their Catholic pastor had refused to give Grandma absolution. Since a good Catholic had to regularly go to confession, my rebellious grandparents traveled eight miles in a horse-drawn buggy to Hillsboro, a small trading center beyond the parish boundary, so Grandma could go to confession once a month on a Saturday afternoon. There, they bought groceries and supplies, went to a Grange dance, stayed overnight, and the next morning, drove back to the church in North Plains. Grandpa, furious with the church, refused any longer to accompany Grandma to Mass and instead took up reading the newspaper while he waited in the buggy.

Grandma's face would light up in a broad smile as she took up the story, "When Leroy, Fritz, and I went to the Communion rail, the priest didn't say a word. You know," she would laugh, "that priest didn't stay too long in the parish after that." I understood that the priest had requested a transfer.

Mysticism

While Grandpa and Grandma's stories emboldened me to question Catholic doctrine, church ritual nurtured and deepened my natural mysticism. From adolescence on, wordless emotion welled up from within me whenever I received Communion. I never understood why I cried; yet the tears continued. It's nothing, I would tell my own small children twenty years later. Don't worry, Mama always cries in church.

Swallowing the Body of Christ, I marveled that God existed in a tiny wafer—for a few minutes, God lived in me! Those moments evoked unrequited longing, planted seeds that would mature into full-blown mysticism and eventually blossom in self-awareness. But not before I endured forty years of sermons exhorting love, obedience, and forgiveness. Perhaps once or twice in all that time, a priest said something that connected with my sense of mystical oneness. Never was my selfhood affirmed. And always the feminine was denigrated. Women just were not good enough. But then, no one was untainted—born in original sin, eternally flawed, every woman and every man had to find their way to forgiveness.

As to the wordless longing, it was not unlike how I expressed all my feelings. I had been taught at a very early age, perhaps during the terrible twos when I threw a tantrum and Mother spanked me for my temper, that feelings could not be expressed. Strong emotions resulted in quiet tears, often without my knowing why. A beautiful sunset, a tale of great sadness, the sight of an old woman gently wiping tears from her husband's eyes, a great victory, the signing of a peace treaty—all brought tears.

On the other hand, I knew I was different. I was the first child; I was big. for my age; I was very bright; I had skipped a grade; other people did not think about the things I thought about. I felt my difference—my isolation from others my age, from my classmates, from belonging—in intensely deep sadness. It did not occur to me that I was chronically depressed.

Chicks

The God of my childhood was a male, an Omniscient Being who permeated Mother's and my life with guilt, judgment, and damnation. A capricious, invisible judge, he loomed everywhere, knew everything, judged everyone, and punished every sin. I took exceptional care never to offend, yet I knew that inevitably I would slip up; I could only hope for mercy. He was the Holy

One—he was Terror, he was Wrath, he was Judgment, and paradoxically, he was Beauty, Goodness, and Love. He—he—he circumscribed every moment and every action of my life.

No matter what I did, no matter what I thought, no matter what I said—no matter how hard I tried—the prospect of banishment to hell loomed before me. As St. Paul said in the Holy Bible, I would grow up to become a woman, the cause of men's sin and damnation.

Not only was I sinful, I was expendable—just as my Aunt Flossie had been when my cousin Pat was born.

In the spring of 1945, one Sunday after Mass, when I was twelve, Mary Lou, Pat, and Pauline—their classmate at Queen of the Angels Catholic School in Portland—and I sprawled on a mound of musty hay in the loft of Grandpa and Grandma Mills' barn. Mary Lou, the oldest, had not begun her period; Pat and I, both physically larger, had begun to menstruate the year before.

"If you got pregnant, would you give up your life for your baby?" Pat asked.

"I don't know," Mary Lou whispered. "We're supposed to."

"I guess I would," I hesitated.

I remembered how in the summer before, I had watched as my godfather, my uncle LeRoy, chopped a hen's head off. Horrified, I saw the chicken body half-run, half-fly in crazy, diminishing circles in the barnyard. Blood spurted from the headless neck onto the bare ground. In a few seconds, the feathered body collapsed, its two legs jutting straight out. From his bent position at the great, round tree block, my uncle had straightened up, swinging the blood-streaked double-bladed axe. From under thick, dark eyebrows, he had glanced at me. Seeing my shock, his laughter echoed across the barren yard.

Now, in the hayloft with my cousins, confusion raced through my mind. *Women are treated like chickens,* I thought. *They tell the doctor to save the baby, not the mother. Men say women are the cause of the downfall of men, like St. Paul said. Men rule the world. Men are like God. God is a man.*

"I hate it," I said to my cousins. "But what choice do I have? If I say no, I'll go to hell. If I say yes, I might die."

A New Name

Lee Pangle, the new physics teacher, appeared as young as some of his students. Just out of college, on his first assignment, he stood at the front of the room handing out papers. "George Mills?" he called.

No one answered.

You could tell Mr. Pangle was trying to make a good impression. He wanted to start his teaching career on a strong foundation and he knew these unruly farm kids could quickly get out of hand. He needed to keep control.

He tried again, "Gee-oh Mills?"

Behind me, a boy snickered. Others laughed out loud. God, he's calling me, I thought! I wrote Geo Mills on my papers because my name, Georgianna, was so long. I was fourteen, shy, the only girl in the class. They were laughing at me, too! Oh, God.

By then, Mr. Pangle was completely frustrated; his face flushed red. He shifted his body position, tried to look stern. It did not help that his voice quivered, "Joe Mills?"

The scions of Vernonia doubled over. Howls of laughter filled the room. I was sitting in the front row. I reached up and took the paper from him.

"That's me," I squeaked.

These skinny farm boys and clever town kids, stars on the football field and basketball court, began to call me Jo. For the next two school years, I helped them with their physics and biology class assignments and envied their breezy confidence. I began to introduce myself as Jo.

Mr. Chipps, a tall, slender man with sandy hair who taught English, was also new that year. He told lots of jokes, taught us to structure sentences, insisted on discipline, and took me under his wing. Working on his master's in psychology, he asked if I would help him administer and grade IQ tests, then correlate them with students' report cards. From James Chipps I learned I had the highest scores of any student in the school, among the top 2 percent nationwide. "Don't worry," he told me. "I know you are unhappy and feel out of place here. There'll be others like you when you get to college."

In my senior year, when I was sixteen, I began to receive scholarship offers. Believing a public university would provide greater educational opportunity and more chances to meet men, I chose the University of Oregon at Eugene. There, warned by the church of the dangers of secular education, I avoided psychology, philosophy, and religion classes (only to take them up twenty-five years later in my master's degree studies). In 1950, near the end of my first year in college, I decided to study political science. I was seventeen years old.

You Can Be President of the United States

Home for Easter vacation in the spring of 1950, at dusk one evening I crossed the gravel road in front of the house, crawled through the barbwire fence, and entered the field where my father guided a plow behind Old Jack. Four months earlier, I had celebrated my seventeenth birthday.

"Dinner in fifteen minutes," I called.

Leaving the scoop blade standing in the rich brown earth, Dad walked forward and began to unhitch the horse. As he undid the harness, he said, "I didn't go to college, but you are—you have a great opportunity."

Holding the reins in one hand, his long legs straddling a loamy furrow, he continued, "When I was a boy, as I walked to school and home again every day, the neighbor kids threw mud at me. They made fun of me, because I was Catholic—called me a Cat Licker. I came home bawling every night." He shifted his belt on his thin frame. "Times have changed," he said. "You don't have to worry about discrimination."

He went on, "This is the greatest country in the world. People here get free education. We're capitalists. Look at me: I don't own much—a horse, a plow, some farm equipment, and part interest with the bank in this land. But it's mine! Nobody's going to take it from me. In America, everyone has a chance."

I held the gate open as he led Old Jack through. His arm swept the air, pointing to the broad expanse of field and forest, "You made it to college," he said. "You can do whatever you want! Why you could be the president of the United States!"

He mounted the horse, crossed the road, and headed toward the barn several hundred yards away. I latched the gate behind him and returned to the house to help dish up supper. *Dad has said the same things all my life, but never in quite the same way. Now,* I marveled, *he treats me like an adult. More—I carry his dreams.*

But I can't be president. Women aren't even in politics. On the other hand, I'm supposed to help people. That's what the voice told me. I don't see how I'll ever be in politics, and I'll sure never be president, but probably I'll be different from other women—I don't know how, but I will be.

That June, I returned home from college. My father took me to Astoria at the mouth of the Columbia River and introduced me to a recruiter at the Union Hall. He asked if I would like to wait tables on the river ferry. Since the Teamsters had jurisdiction over the river and the AFL had responsibility for waitresses, I joined both the International Teamsters Union and the

American Federation of Labor's Waitress Union. For three summers, boarding with old family friends, Aunt Mayme and Uncle John Miner, I waited tables and short-order cooked aboard the ferries that crossed the mouth of the Columbia River. I worked hard, but it was a good job and paid well. I earned enough to pay my share of tuition and books, and to pay for my clothing and incidentals during the school year.

Smart Woman

By my eighteenth birthday, in November 1950, I clearly knew my subsidiary place in society. Women were measured by their beauty and pleasing manner, not by their ability to think. Recalling those college years, from 1949 to 1953, my dreams of meeting and marrying a tall, blonde college graduate, a devout Catholic who would inherit family wealth and go into the family business, whose IQ and grade point exceeded mine, now seem grandiose and foolish. None of the men I dated were even Catholic; I dreamed of Prince Charming, but I understood that if I married at all, I would have to settle for less.

If I did not marry, I daydreamed I would work in the United States Embassy in France. To prepare for that eventuality, I took French and studied international politics; always practical, I completed typing and stenography classes as well.

When I applied for one of the most prestigious scholarships offered at the university—covering full tuition, books, and expenses for my senior year—I falsified my motive for attending college. I wrote what I thought the committee would want to hear. I wanted to learn; I wanted to succeed; but I told them that as an educated woman, I would rear successful sons and daughters, contributing members of society. I did not mention a possible political career.

In winter 1952, toward the end of my junior year, I received a call from a university official telling me that I was a finalist and was to interview with a woman on the scholarship board. When we met, the woman—an exquisitely coiffured, perfectly made-up socialite wearing a fur jacket and dripping with diamonds—told me that she was late for another meeting. As we walked rapidly toward the Student Union building, I felt like a farm waif, poverty stricken and inadequate. Nevertheless, I made my pitch on the run, telling her how I would use the award and what a difference it would make in my life.

Cutting me off in mid-sentence, she exclaimed, "Mah deah, don't you know? You'ah it!" Before I could thank her properly, she rushed away.

Dazed, I crossed the street to sit on an icy stone bench near a winterized fountain. In the center bowl, a graceful nymph poised, mouth open, waiting for speech. Inside me, spring had arrived; joy gushed, bubbled, and soared. I had won!

I returned that summer to Astoria to live with John and Mayme Miner. There I would wait tables and short-order cook aboard the ferries that crossed the mouth of the Columbia River for a third year.

On a balmy mid-June afternoon in 1952, soon after my junior year in college finished, six months before my twentieth birthday, Aunt Mayme and I were thinning carrots in her garden in the backyard. The conversation turned to my after-college plans. Straightening up from a row of feathery green tops, Aunt Mayme wiped her brow and smoothed back her tightly permed, salt and pepper hair. As she surveyed the yard and the street beyond, she remarked stolidly, "You'll never get a man—men don't like smart women."

NINETEEN TO TWENTY-SIX (SUMMER 1952–1959) COURTSHIP AND MARRIAGE

Shortly after Aunt Mayme's bruising pronouncement, I met Stan Garceau. An enlisted man in the United States Navy stationed at Tongue Point Naval Station, he boarded the ferry one afternoon and ordered a hamburger with a fried egg on it. He was on his way to Yakima for the Fourth of July to see his family.

We bantered back and forth, and before he left to drive the car he had borrowed from a friend off the ferry, he asked for my phone number. Wiping the counter and putting away the dish he had used, I casually asked the sailor he had been with, "What's that guy's name?"

"Oh," he said, "that's Stan, the man, the leader of the band!"

After Stan phoned to ask me out, I began to attend the USO dances where Stan and the naval band played every Friday and Saturday night. He looked great in his uniform. Stan played first trumpet in the sixteen-piece naval orchestra and was a superb musician, especially fond of and good at Dixieland jazz. A good-looking man with curly brown hair and startlingly clear blue eyes, born on October 26, 1926, he was six years older than I. He had been baptized Catholic as an infant and attended eleven grades of Catholic schools in Yakima, Washington before enlisting in the navy at seventeen near at the end of the Second World War. He mustered out of the navy when the war ended and attended college for two years before dropping out. Then he played in bands in the Yakima Valley for several years before reenlisting in the navy a year or two before we met. He was the first Catholic

I dated, and since I had always been told that I should marry a Catholic, he had an advantage over any prior boyfriend.

It would be years before I studied astrology and became aware that both our natal Suns were in Scorpio, a sexually passionate location, but one subject to hidden drives for power as well as frequent moodiness. My Aries Moon/Uranus conjunction eventually proved to be a serious detriment to the marriage: Stan was looking for a wife and mother for his children; I was born independent, meant to be a pioneer in new fields. I sought a conscious, equal partnership; he searched for a conventional Catholic wife and marriage. He was not the tall, blonde, intellectual man I had dreamed of, but he was amusing and talkative. In 1952, when we met, I was nineteen and he was twenty-five. The country was between wars.

In that summer of 1952, ours was a hurry-up romance, but not exactly a wartime courtship. A decade had not yet passed since the end of the Second World War and the country was always on alert to the Russian threat. Stan would be leaving in the fall on a new assignment with the navy, and I would be returning to school. Our Scorpio suns fell passionately in love, and in a few short weeks, we agreed to marry.

That fall, before Stan transferred to Long Beach, California, and I returned to school, he gave me a ring and took me to Yakima to meet his parents. We wrote regularly and, between classes at the university, I began planning for a June wedding the following year.

Déjà Vu

Talking with friends in the student lounge one afternoon in the spring before I married, suddenly I experienced myself as simultaneously two separate beings. One of me spoke; the other witnessed what I said and knew what my friend Dianna would answer. The experience lasted a few seconds; as quickly as it had begun, I returned to ordinary consciousness.

"You guys!" I exclaimed, "Jim was talking about Civil War politics, I started to answer, and all at once, I felt like I was two different people. We'd all been here before, saying the same things!"

"Something like that happened to me once," Jim said. "A deer leaped onto the road. Dad swerved, and as the car rolled, I watched from twenty feet above." He'd had some sort of out-of-body experience, watching himself from a distance as events unfolded.

Dianna confided, "Three years ago, when I had pneumonia, I left my body and floated down the hospital corridor. I looked into several rooms where children were sleeping." She hesitated, then said, "I had a choice. I didn't have to come back into my body, but I thought about my mom, and I came back."

I felt reassured. I wasn't losing my mind. Nor was I ill, nor had I been in an accident. My experience was simply uncomfortable split awareness—probably the *déjà vu* I had read about. Still, that curious feeling of being two people at once, observer and observed, speaker and listener, didn't make sense to me.

For weeks, as I attended classes and arranged wedding details, I puzzled over my identity. I seemed to be a different person depending on whom I was with and where I was. I was an American, a Roman Catholic, and the daughter of Oregon pioneers; I was a friend, a student, and a fiancée. I was happy or sad; I longed for things to be better. Yet, beyond ephemeral roles and states of mind, I thought there must be an enduring, essential Jo.

The Baltimore Catechism, the official manual of Catholic doctrine, said I was a separate, unique being, created by God to know him, to love him, and to serve him. Eventually, I would die and my soul would separate from my body to go to heaven or hell, depending on my action and God's mysterious will.

I sensed that my soul—my enduring, essential self—had fleetingly appeared in the Student Union. In that time of transition, as I moved from one feminine role to another—from being single to being married, I wondered why she had appeared and how—and who—she was. For forty years, she would elude me.

I'll Dig Ditches for You

That spring, because Stan wanted me to be in Long Beach, his ship's homeport, while he was on an eight-month tour of the Pacific, I refused a prestigious graduate fellowship in the University of Oregon's Political Science Department. I suppose any young woman today would accept the fellowship, especially when her fiancé would be out of the country for nearly a year. In 1952, women, especially Catholic women, did what their man asked them to do. We were at their beck and call, responding to their changing moods and implied wishes. We were taught to be loving helpmates. Difficult as it is for today's youth to fathom, women had no life independent of their husband and children—and certainly no career.

Less than a year after Stan and I met, we married. After an evening wedding rehearsal, Stan and I sat talking in my parents' car. Looking out through the windshield over a darkened hayfield, across the valley of the Nehalem River, we saw a meteor arc across the sky above the line of hills directly to the north.

Pointing to its trajectory, I confided, for the first time to anyone, my sense of life mission. "I've always known there was something—I don't know what exactly—I must do for many people. Whatever it turns out to be, I could flash and burn like that shooting star. Are you sure—really sure—you want to marry me?"

"I'll dig ditches for you," Stan answered.

Obedient to Your Husband

We returned to my parents' home to meet Father Emil Kies, Mother's second cousin from Portland, who would conduct the wedding ceremony the following morning. That night, in what was then the customary prenuptial interview conducted by Catholic priests, Father Kies enunciated Catholic doctrine: "Marriage is a holy sacrament. You may enjoy one another sexually, but you must never avoid having children. You may not use birth control. Do nothing to avoid pregnancy."

For me, Father Kies had special instructions: "Be obedient to your husband, Christ's representative in the home. Never refuse to have sex with him."

His instructions were actually quite liberal for the time. The church had earlier taught that sex was for procreation only. He was telling us we could enjoy being with one another! But only if we intended to have children.

Twenty-five years later, my parents would tell me that when they were courting, Dad had said, "I want our children—boys and girls—raised and educated the same. No woman should be dependent on a man." They encouraged me to be independent, yet they never spoke of options other than marriage. For a proper Catholic woman, none existed. They could not have imagined the conflict I would experience as an educated woman, self-sufficient in a society where women were obedient and acquiescent, dependent on men and society for meaning and purpose.

The night before the wedding, Stan's parents came with his brother, Allen, who was best man, to stay at our country home. On the following morning, a bright and clear Saturday in mid-June 1953, Father Kies married us at a Mass in the small mission church in Birkenfeld, Oregon. Family and friends from both my mother's and my father's sides of the family drove from near Portland, an hour and a half away, to attend.

I wore a lovely, shantung white suit dress and veil my mother had made for me; Stan wore his United States Navy uniform. My godchild and sister, Lucile, was flower girl; my cousin, Pat, was the bride's maid. Moved by the profound commitment I was making, an irrevocable life decision, I remember most that I cried throughout the ceremony. The tears embarrassed me, but I could not stop crying.

After the ceremony, our one hundred guests drove two miles to the reception held in our family yard. Mother and my younger sisters served casseroles and salads, and of course the wedding cake. My grandmother Mills, the one who often reminded me to remember who I was, took me aside to tell me that she had cried at her own wedding. It was a good sign, she said; her marriage had already lasted fifty years.

Stan and I borrowed the family car and drove twenty miles to a small motel on the coast highway for our honeymoon night. I remember the joy of sanctioned sexuality offset by the meanness of the room we rented. The next morning, we rose early, drove back to my parents' home, picked them up, and drove four hours to Eugene, Oregon for my college graduation ceremony, then another four hours home to Birkenfeld.

Because Stan was on a short shore leave and we had little money, we stayed in a room above the garage at my parents' home for the next several days. Followed around by my five curious little sisters, we helped with the farming chores. Of all the improbable things we did on our honeymoon, the most unique was tromping silage for all of one day.

We left then on the Greyhound bus for a long ride to Long Beach, California, where Stan's ship, the *USS Small* was in dock. Assuming the role women had occupied for centuries, I embarked on the path of subservience.

First Argument

Three weeks after we married, Stan's ship sailed from Long Beach, California, bound for Japan and an eight-month tour of the Pacific. We corresponded, of course, but his letters were sporadic, depending on the overseas postal service. Apart from my husband, in a strange city far from family and the rural life I had grown up in, I was very lonely.

While Stan was overseas, I lived with a college friend in Glendale and worked as an insurance clerk in downtown Los Angeles. I was used to rain, not heat and smog-filled skies. Five months after I moved to California, it finally rained. Cleta, the college friend with whom I was sharing an apartment, woke me at midnight when she returned from work. In the dark, outside our second-story apartment, I leaned against the iron porch railing in a nylon nightgown and cried as the rain soaked my gown. I loved the rain.

When Stan returned the following February, he was a stranger. How was I supposed to be with this man I had not seen in eight months? In a few days, things settled down. In another month, I quit my insurance job and we moved to Mare Island, north of San Francisco, where his ship went into dry dock. Young and in love, we economized, surviving on $145 a month, the pittance an enlisted man and his dependent wife received from the United States government.

One summer afternoon, we sweltered in our apartment on the second floor of a hastily built, government-furnished four-plex. Around the complex, radios blared and a child wailed on the lawn below.

"Let's go for a walk," I said. "Maybe we can buy an ice cream cone at the PX."

"You go, I don't have any money," Stan answered.

"But you just got paid," I said.

"I bought drinks for the guys last night."

"You spent a month's pay?"

"I only had ten dollars."

"What happened to the other eighty?" I swallowed tears.

"I paid a couple loans."

I pressed for details; he became silent. I had read the advice columns and studied how to be a good Catholic wife—how to keep your husband happy. I knew this discussion was important; how we handled our first disagreement would set the pattern for our future life together. I thought, *Okay, don't speak; that's fine. I'm too upset and angry to be coherent.*

Lying on the sagging bed that came with the apartment, I sobbed. *I want to be a good wife. I should be supportive, not nagging ... maybe God will help.*

I got up, splashed cold water on my eyes, and went into the kitchen where big band music still played.

"Honey," I apologized, "I'm sorry I asked. It's just that I don't know how we're going to buy groceries. I don't know what we'll do for a month."

He reached over to the radio and turned the knob. The music blared. Over the bleat of a brassy trumpet, I shouted, "Stan, I'm really sorry!"

A good Scorpio, Stan did not speak for twenty-four hours. He had found the key to my submission, a punishing silence he would use again and again during the thirty-plus years of our marriage. Unable to bear the loss of love, I capitulated. And, blaming the military for the low pay Stan received and expecting that when he was a civilian, his income would improve, I failed to see a developing pattern. I would excuse his inability to provide for his family for all the years we were together.

When the USS *Small* returned to Long Beach, I found another job—secretary to an oil refinery superintendent—holding it until my first pregnancy showed, then quitting as the law required. Stan mustered out of the navy; three weeks before our first child was born, he injured his back.

When Paul was ten days old, Stan and I visited the home of navy friends. Stan got out of the car, body bent at an angle. He walked around to the passenger side, took the baby from me, and led the way up a wide, concrete walkway bordered with red geraniums. He had gone only a few feet when he groaned and doubled over, almost dropping Paul.

Taking the baby from Stan, I watched as he, in obvious pain, continued up two flights of stairs. Climbing slowly behind him, carrying Paul, the diaper bag, and my purse, panicked thoughts rose with me. *God, what are we going to do? I feel so sorry for Stan; we talked about having four or five children ... I can't go back to work for another six weeks, I can't draw unemployment, and we're broke. God, I don't want to support us all our lives ... I hope I don't injure myself ... I can't be sick, too. Paul and Stan need me.*

A few weeks later, both Stan and I hired on at North American Aviation; a woman friend cared for Paul. A year later, Stan became a cargo handler for Alaska Airlines. Shortly after our second child, Suzanne, was born, at Stan's request, Alaska transferred him to Seattle.

We were both eager to return to the Northwest, closer to both families, back in familiar country, but as we drove north, the airline's pilots began a strike that would last nearly six months. In the interim, we alternated stays with both families in our childhood homes, a difficult time for all of us.

As a Catholic, to avoid another pregnancy, I practiced the church-approved rhythm method of birth control. I did not think I would become pregnant while nursing my second child, but three months after Suzanne's birth, I was disappointed that I was expecting again.

When the airline strike ended, we moved into a duplex in Renton, Washington, and Stan went back to work. For the next year, I was a full-time housewife, the longest period in my life that I did not work outside the home. We ate lots of hamburger casseroles, and I cared for the children and watched TV game shows. I was bored. Stan's income was barely enough for the family to get by.

Politics and Spirituality

Twenty-Six to Thirty-Two (1959–1964) Politics

In September 1959, nine months after the birth of my third child, Warren, I returned to full-time work as an executive secretary at the Boeing Company in Renton, Washington. I was pleased to be active again in the world, happier than I had been at home caring for small children and watching TV game shows day after day. My neighbor friend, Barbara Schellert, commented that my home was much cleaner when I worked than it had been when I was home all the time. That December, a month after my twenty-seventh birthday, I joined the local Republican club.

"Can I go to a political meeting a week from Wednesday?" I waited until the children were in bed to ask.

"Who's going to watch the kids?" Stan replied.

"I was hoping you would. I'll get them ready for bed—and I'll only be gone a couple hours."

"Let me think about it."

I waited a day or two before asking again. This time Stan agreed that I could go to the meeting.

That fall, I went door-to-door with other club members, handing out brochures for a congressional candidate. He did not win, but I had learned a great deal about local politics and I was eager for more involvement. I had graduated in political science at the University of Oregon; campaigning was an exhilarating and demanding process that spoke to my sense of life commitment. After the election, finding none of us in the club agreed on the sequence of campaign events, I began to keep a journal, a practice I continued for forty years.

41

Looking through my early journals, I find no spiritual notes, no philosophical questions, and no mention of feelings, yet I vividly remember the sea of unarticulated emotion in which I lived. I had a hazy awareness of self-continuity intimately connected to something greater: God, I supposed. I vaguely sensed the unity of all things. Although I never spoke of it, the mission I first knew at eight was always close to consciousness, a compelling awareness of my life somehow directed toward an undefined task. *When would I begin my real work?*

Washington State legislators, as is customary throughout the United States, are elected from legislative districts, each with local voting precincts. Individuals run as political party candidates for precinct leader positions representing the various political parties recognized by the state. In November, I had been elected as a precinct leader. In December 1960, precinct leaders elected me vice chairman of Washington State's Forty-seventh Legislative District Republican Party.

The following April, eager to actually see the state capitol, Stan and I took a midweek day off and drove to Olympia, taking the two younger children with us. Paul, our eldest child, was in school and we would return in time to meet his bus.

The legislature was not in session; we arrived in the late morning to find the public rooms closed. But fortune, or perhaps the divine spirit, was on our side. As we stood on a balcony overlooking the rotunda, a man appeared and asked if he could help us. Explaining we had left our oldest child in school and driven down for the day, he offered to give us a private tour.

He took us to the gallery above the Senate floor, showed us the offices behind the chambers, and related the history of the building. We stood outside the governor's office and admired the entry, then visited the secretary of state's office across the way. When he took us onto the floor of the House of Representatives, I stood on the red-carpeted side aisle looking out upon the desks used by legislators during session. Our guide stepped onto the inclined floor into the chamber.

"You can come down," the man said, inviting us onto the floor.

As I stepped out, I wondered in surprise at the incline beneath my feet—the floor was actually a slightly concave bowl.

Simultaneously, my inner voice spoke: *You will work here.*

Although this was the first occurrence of the voice in more than twenty years, even after that long passage of time, I knew that I had found my life work—in politics, in the capitol building.

ॐ

For the next three years, while directing party activities, I campaigned for local and state candidates. Under the auspices of Toastmasters International, in which only men were members, Henry, his wife, Barbara, and I came up with the idea of enrolling women, using our initials instead of our full names. Barbara and I convinced other women to join, and we began practicing to speak in public.

In August 1963, thrilled with an invitation to a statewide organizing meeting, I signed on to help elect Dan Evans, a King County legislator, as Washington's governor. Several weeks later, Jim Dolliver, state campaign director, later executive director of the governor's office, asked me to become vice chairman of the Evans legislative district campaign. Because women did not serve as campaign chairs, while I ran the organization, Jim and I searched for a businessman to be the chairman.

Before we found him, I became pregnant with my fourth child. Full of regret for lost opportunity—few women engaged in politics and pregnant women never did—I called a woman friend, a member of the state campaign steering committee, to resign my position. As luck would have it, she was also expecting; we agreed that both of us would continue campaigning. A few weeks later, a Bellevue businessman became the legislative district campaign chairman.

In the mid-sixties, the foundations of the conservative Christian Republican Party were just being established, a counterbalance to the emerging social revolution with its liberal agenda. Young people today cannot grasp how different the country has become. The 1960's struggle was immense, the beginning of a fight for the soul of a nation. The Christian Conservative Movement morphed and grew for thirty-five years, culminating in the bitter, national political schism that occurred during the 2000 election. Much has changed; sixties conservatives have become the liberals of today's Republican Party.

In 1964, Goldwater conservatives accused my friend Henry Schellert, who was running for the Renton city council, of being soft on Communism. I complained to the spokesman for the John Birch Society, the most right wing of the conservative organizations, a man who was ostensibly my political friend. My ploy failed; speaking for Henry backfired. Word passed among my conservative political friends that I could not be trusted. Determined to win the argument, I redoubled my efforts to elect liberal party members as delegates to the state convention.

Three weeks prior to delivering my fourth child at age thirty-two, I would have preferred to stay home from that year's Legislative District Caucus. As leader of the liberal Republicans, I needed to attend the meeting. Purposely sitting in the exact middle of the local theater where the meeting was held, so that I could feel the mood of the gathering and rally my troops, I watched as the conservatives trounced the liberals, winning vote after vote. When old political friends cast ballots against me for delegate to the state convention, a position I had held the four previous years, my spirits plummeted. Nominated for alternate delegate, I was again defeated.

I prepared to leave the auditorium. As I pulled my coat over my bulging belly, a member of the Evans Campaign Committee asked me if I minded if she nominated me for a seat on the King County Platform Committee. "No, don't bother," I told her. "The conservatives have the votes, they'll just beat me again."

"Let me try," she pleaded.

"Okay," I said, suppressing tears. *What does it matter?*

As it turned out, I held the deciding vote on the platform committee of the most populated and influential county in the state. Feeling sorry for me, my old conservative friends had voted me into what they thought was an inconsequential position. The Goldwater forces had forfeited their opportunity to shape state party policy that year.

My Baby Lives and We Win the Election

After Greg's birth in May 1965, I worked as a secretary to Boeing's chief engineer on the Supersonic Transport project. In the evenings and on weekends, I directed the Evans for Governor legislative campaign.

My new baby was allergic to cow's milk, but having dealt with a similar condition with Suzanne, my second child, I expected no difficulty. When Greg was five months old, his allergic wheeze developed overnight into a serious cold and he was admitted to the hospital near our home. Early the next morning, a day I will never forget, Halloween 1964, the doctor called. "Mrs. Garceau," he said, "Gregory has pneumonia. He should be moved immediately to Seattle Children's Hospital."

The siren screamed as the ambulance raced fifteen miles to the hospital on the northwest shore of Lake Washington. Riding in the back of the vehicle with Greg, whose face was turning blue, I prayed. Stan met us at the hospital, and together we waited through five fear-filled hours. Finally, the attending physician gave us the results of numerous tests.

"Greg is in critical condition," he said. "He has double pneumonia, laryngitis, bronchitis, and ear infections. Medical science isn't advanced enough to tell whether he has a viral or a bacterial infection, so we're treating him for both." He paused. "We're doing everything we can—but I can't promise he'll live. Come any time, day or night—and pray—all we can do now is pray."

In a downpour that evening, unwilling to disappoint my three older children, I accompanied them on trick-or-treat rounds. Hiding my fear that Greg was dying, silently crying, I moved in and out of shadows where ghosts and skeletons darted, praying my baby would live.

On Sunday evening, after the longest twenty-four hours of my life, the doctor phoned, "Gregory's temperature has broken," he said. "If his heart holds out, he'll make it."

A chance! Oh, God, a chance!

Each time Stan and I visited the hospital, I listened to Greg's labored breathing; minute-by-minute, hour-by-hour, I feared he would die. Stressed to the breaking point, still I could not tell anyone about the invisible angel with outstretched wings who hovered behind me. *Maybe it's St. Michael, the Archangel. If I say anything, people will think I'm mad.* My head spun, I feared I'd lose consciousness. "If anything happens," I told Stan, "get me to a doctor." I could not tell him about the angel; he would laugh and dismiss my concern that I might be losing my mind. I knew he cared about Greg, but he would say I was just being silly.

Greg lay under an oxygen tent, barely holding on to life, heart pounding so hard his chest moved up and down with every beat. A tiny paper cup covered an incision in his fontanel where a feeding tube had been inserted. On the table beside the crib, an instrument for performing a laryngectomy rested, ready for the medical staff to grab if his breathing stopped. Each time I entered the room, I checked to see if the surgical tool was still there.

On election night, before obligatory appearances at campaign headquarters, Stan and I visited Greg. The oxygen tent had been removed; the tool to perform a laryngectomy was gone. As I sat in a rocking chair, a nurse placed my swaddled child in my arms. For the first time in eight days, I held my son. He had lost one-third of his body weight, but he would live.

From a speakerphone mounted on the wall above my head, a radio announcer's voice filled the room, "Dan Evans, leading by a hundred thousand votes, is winning by a landslide."

Oh, God, my child is alive! We've won the election! The campaign I devoted my waking hours to for eighteen months has succeeded. My baby is alive! There will never be another day like this. Nothing as significant could ever happen again.

Although the new moon in Scorpio that evening brought a new start for my son and a new beginning for the state of Washington, Greg's childhood illness weakened his body. Years would pass before we understood the full impact on his life and eventually on mine. The souls of mothers and children are always intimately linked—but to what extent is usually not so clear.

Thirty-Two to Thirty-Nine (1964–1971)
Taking Responsibility
The Move to Spokane

Shortly after Gregory's release from the hospital, the accordion school where Stan worked part-time asked him to start a new branch. In January 1965, he moved to Spokane, Washington, to start the accordion school; in June, the children and I followed.

Finding work in Spokane was a challenge. Not only were salaries lower than in Seattle, nearly all positions were placed through employment agencies, requiring the payment of expensive fees. The family would depend on my income while the school developed. My spirits hit bottom when the prestigious *Spokesman Review*, Spokane's daily newspaper, one of the largest employers in the city, refused to interview me. Company policy prohibited hiring married women because the owner believed mothers should be at home with their children. After several weeks of searching, I accepted a 25 percent reduction in salary and became executive assistant to the AAA club manager.

Birth Control

For several years while we were in Seattle and after our move to Spokane, I had been under severe emotional stress because of our financial situation. I constantly worried about becoming pregnant again, going bankrupt, and losing our home. Eventually I developed a hormone imbalance. When my doctor prescribed birth control pills, Father Michaelson, our pastor, gave permission for me to take the medicine "as long as the condition continues."

Outwardly compliant, inwardly I seethed. Not only was I the primary breadwinner for the family, the church demanded that I bear child after child. Furious, I asked myself why single men who were priests made decisions about the lives of married women. *What's moral about a husband expecting unprotected sex whenever he wants it? He's beyond reproach, yet I'm told I will go to hell if I refuse to have sex with my husband.*

Father Michaelson could be grudging if he wished. The church had its rules, but my body had circumvented them. I would never again have unprotected sex.

Letters to Olympia/Spokane Politics

From Spokane, I wrote to my friend from the Evans campaign. She forwarded my letters to Slade Gorton, a King County legislator and to Governor Dan Evans. Both men would eventually go on to be United States senators. When Slade visited Spokane, he introduced me to other Republican legislators and party members. Some time that year, I met with Bill Jacobs, a representative from the governor's office and made several proposals.

Long after we all left office, I attended an eightieth birthday party for Governor Dan Evans. There I met Bill again. He told me he had taken my proposals back to Olympia after we met and had recommended that I be hired. For forty years, I had not known this.

Some months after our move to Spokane, a political acquaintance mentioned me to Bill Treadwell, a newly hired Gonzaga University law professor who wanted to run for Congress. Bill had no connections in Spokane. When he invited me to lunch, he asked me to run his campaign against Tom Foley, the popular Democrat leader of the United States House of Representatives. I advised him to spend some time in the community, get to know people, make political friends. An unknown running against a long-time, highly respected Democrat had no chance of winning a race for Congress.

A few months later, calculating that Bill Treadwell would lose his bid for office, but I would gain invaluable political contacts, I agreed to co-manage the Treadwell for Congress campaign. The following year, as a member of the mayor's campaign steering committee, I helped elect Dave Rodgers mayor of Spokane.

Meanwhile, my husband's accordion school did not attract the students he'd hoped for and finally folded. Puzzling about what to do, on a sunny autumn afternoon in 1967, I walked on a path under the High Bridge west of the city. Below the winding trail that wound through yellowing knee-high grass, brightly colored bushes lined the lazy Spokane River. Here and there, a startled bird flew up ahead of me, the flutter of wings breaking the sleepy silence. As I progressed along the path, I wrestled with the truth of my fourteen-year marriage.

According to the Catholic Church, a man is the head of the family. Women are dependent on them for protection and financial support. Yet, in the fourteen years of my marriage, I've provided most of the income.

On the other hand, I want the marriage to continue. I've been crying a lot, hiding my sadness from him and the children, but that doesn't resolve anything. And it sure doesn't pay bills.

I'm thirty-five years old. I need to accept life as it is. Contrary to what the church says, I have to take responsibility—for him, for the children, and for the marriage—and make my decisions accordingly.

Later that month, the intense psychological pressure that I was under climaxed. I was on my way to work an overtime assignment in inventory when, only a few blocks from home, my body began to shake uncontrollably. I was very frightened; nothing like it had ever happened to me. What was happening? Bringing the car to a stop beside the curb, I calmed myself. When the shaking subsided, I returned home and arranged to see a doctor, who told me I was about to have a nervous breakdown. My adrenalin levels were so high that I functioned as though I were in a war zone. He prescribed tranquillizers and I slept for days.

That fall, when Stan said he wanted to look for work in western Washington, I said that I would like to stay in Spokane until after the 1968 gubernatorial election. He agreed.

The following spring, I landed my first paid political position as director of the Spokane County Dan Evans Reelection Committee. It was a heady time. When I think about that campaign, I remember the success we had and how wonderful it was to marshal the efforts of others to a cause we believed in. At the height of that year's campaign, I directed over five hundred volunteers.

I especially remember a call from a young volunteer at Seattle headquarters. He asked how many brochures to send for the last week's doorbelling campaign, a time when a political candidate's literature is delivered to every home in the voting area.

"Fifty thousand," I said. The number of brochures I requested would allow a thorough leaflet saturation drop in all marginal precincts. I had the volunteers lined up and I knew the area well. Fifty thousand was a phenomenal number and flyers were expensive to produce, but I felt we should leave them on every doorstep.

He gasped, "There's no way."

"That's what I need. I've got four hundred twenty-five people in the field; that's what I need. If you can't handle it, let me speak to Peter (the state campaign manager).

I got the brochures. And we delivered every one of them.

Governor's Assistant

After the election, we moved to Olympia, the capitol of Washington State. I worked briefly in the Department of Motor Vehicles, then as secretary to State Representative Alan Bleuchel. In July 1969, I joined the governor's staff as assistant for correspondence. The following spring, Governor Dan Evans asked me to screen and recommend candidates for state boards and commissions. The governor had asked me to find qualified experts and to consult both Republicans and Democrats. We had reviewed the list of candidates together.

Shortly after my first selection was announced, I received a phone call. "You didn't ask me!" a state representative from western Washington shouted. The receiver rattled, "You can't go over my head!"

"I'm sorry," I tried to soothe the irate legislator. "I didn't know you had a recommendation."

"I'll have your job!" he bellowed. Nothing I said appeased him.

Fearing I had harmed the governor's long-term political prospects, that evening I furiously uprooted weeds from the flowerbeds in our backyard. The next day, when I discussed the legislator's call with Governor Evans, his voice was mild, "John gets hot about everything. He'll get over it."

Catholic Charismatic

That evening, as if prompted by an unseen entity, an acquaintance from our new parish invited me to a meeting where a Seattle nun described a growing, nationwide prayer movement. Around the country, Catholics and Protestants were praying together, calling on the Holy Spirit. In these Charismatic prayer groups, ordinary people were filled with the Holy Spirit just as St. Luke had reported among first-century Christians. Like the whispered-about Pentecostals, the Charismatics sang, praised the Lord, and spoke in tongues.

Taking a book about the movement home with me, I crawled into bed beside my sleeping husband. By penlight, I read inspiring stories of contemporary Christians filled with the Holy Spirit. Well after midnight, I closed the book. *God, I prayed, if this is what you want, I'd like to speak in tongues.*

Abruptly, a torrent of foreign syllables flowed from my mouth, not so loud as to wake my sleeping husband, but dramatic enough to shift my self-awareness. I was pleased and perplexed; what did it all mean? Speaking suddenly in tongues was quite amazing, but I would have to be cautious. I did not want to be fooled. If it were a blessing from God, I was pleased—for I was sure prayer would support my political work.

Thinking back on that time, from the perspective of nearly forty years, I am still amazed at the synchronicity of the invitation to the prayer meeting.

It came just at the time that I faced my first real political test; it seemed meant to be. My spirituality was supporting my involvement in politics.

I had been a Catholic since childhood, attending Mass weekly, following for the most part the tenets of the Catholic Church—albeit wavering largely in my decisions to practice birth control and to be the family breadwinner. Suddenly, I found myself in a role I had never dreamed of: assistant to the governor—not a secretary, but a full-fledged assistant responsible for choosing and appointing citizens of the state to important roles in government.

True, I had always been a mystic. I read everything I could find on the lives of Catholic saints and mystics, and I felt a deep calling to deeper connection with the divine. I longed for a love not of this world. But I was practical, too, assessing as highly improbable the likelihood of finding such a blessed tenderness.

Now unexpectedly in a position of leadership never before held by a woman, fearful that I would make a huge political mistake, the Holy Spirit (as I then thought of the Divine Feminine) had come to my aid in the form of an invitation to attend a Charismatic prayer group. In a synchronous event, on the same day that the legislator had yelled at my performance, I had been invited to a Charismatic prayer meeting—and that had resulted in my sudden speaking in tongues. Politics and spirituality for me were inextricably bound together and would continue so for the eight years I served as assistant and cabinet director in Washington State.

It is said that when the student is ready, the teacher appears. Carl Jung, the Swiss psychologist who coined the word "synchronicity," might have said that my powerful emotional response to the legislator's phone call elicited the invitation to the prayer group.

In the group, I learned that interpretation of tongues and prophecy are separate gifts; one never occurred without the other. In a prayer meeting, a person speaking in tongues might have no idea what she or he spoke, but in the silence that followed a message, another person always interpreted. This is called prophecy. He or she would say something as simple as, "The Lord is with us! He bids us be patient in tribulation, binding up the sick and comforting the bereaved." Delivered in the presence of twenty or thirty devout believers, utterances one would never communicate in ordinary life seemed to carry profound meaning.

With four or five other members of the prayer group steering committee, I led weekly meetings, coordinated the group, and prayed with individuals. In turn, the group provided me with emotional and spiritual support as I embraced my new political role.

Politically, in the right place at the right time as the new wave of feminism crested, I came into my power. In the following seven years, I selected and appointed more than seven thousand women and men from every race, creed, and color to public office. Working to improve the lives of voiceless millions, speaking on behalf of women's issues, I believed I was fulfilling the promise made by my inner voice so many years before. My work impacted the more than 2.5 million citizens of Washington. For the first time since leaving college, I felt validated, both in politics and in the Charismatic Movement.

One with the Universe

The year after our move to Olympia, we purchased camping equipment for the entire family. Every year, we visited Pacific Northwest national parks and historic sites. One summer, when my husband could not accompany us, I took the children and ventured alone to remote Olympic National Park.

There, one morning in a thick fog, I walked at tide's edge. At Kalalock Creek, as I waded the chilly water at the evanescent line where stream met rippling tide, a concave seashell with a tiny hole at its center rolled to rest at my feet. I leaned over to pick it up.

As I straightened, my boundaries vanished. For a mini-second, sea, sky, sand, shell, and I merged. Later that day, sitting on the seashore while my children played nearby, I attempted to capture my feeling:

> *One with the universe,*
> *One with love,*
> *One with stillness by the sea.*
> *The rings of my shell expand out infinitely*
> *Returning light, transcendence and peace*
> *In an ambience of fog.*
> *Half on land and half at sea*
> *Suspended between.*
> *Knowing, sharing, caring.*
> *Thou.*

I had lost myself and felt a blissful unity. As my poem attempted to describe, I had momentarily lost a sense of personal self and become one with the entirety of creation. I experienced joy and awe, a completion beyond anything I had ever conceived of. I had always been a mystic, but nothing in the Catholic Church or my usual activities prepared me for this sense of wholeness, as ephemeral and evanescent as it was. I began seeking ways to duplicate the ecstatic oneness of that brief moment; focused on transcendence, on the space beyond my ego self, my prayer life deepened.

ॐ

Months after that seashore trip, in my office in the governor's suite, I studied a proposed piece of legislation. Responding to a knock, I called, "Come in." Paul Meyer, a Department of Social and Health Services consultant, had stopped by to invite me to lunch at the Presbyterian Church a block away. A men's prayer group he belonged to was sponsoring speakers with discussions that followed for businessmen and church and state leaders. He wanted to know if I would represent the governor's office.

After attending several meetings, I joined the organizing committee, the only woman and the second Roman Catholic in the group. Meeting on alternate Tuesdays, we planned the public meetings. For several years after the luncheons ended, Paul Meyer, Jim Symons and Paul McCann—both Presbyterian ministers, Roger Kuhrt—a Unitarian minister, Bob Benson—the state printer, and I would continue to meet. Paul Meyer became a confidante; we shared so much that eventually our parish priest told me that Paul and I performed the Sacrament of Reconciliation for one another.

I Think for Myself

Three years after I joined the governor's staff, one Saturday morning, as I smoothed the antique white spread on my husband's and my high-canopied bed, I mused about a front-page story in the Catholic newspaper, once again forbidding birth control. *I'm thirty-nine years old, mother of four children, two of them in high school, one in middle school, and the youngest in second grade. The church still demands that I have unprotected sex.*

These were familiar thoughts, but then a startling new idea suddenly occurred to me: *I depend on priests not only for what to think, but how to think. The fundamental shame lies in submissive thinking.*

The more I thought about it, the angrier I became. I was a special assistant to a governor, powerful in my own right, and still I followed the direction of a man who lived in Italy and didn't give a damn whether I lived or died. Well! Just as I had assumed responsibility for the family, I would think for myself!

You Are the Model

I spent long hours at the office, cared for home and children, and attended school and church activities. During these years, Stan was employed with the county road department. We shared household chores; he vacuumed and helped with the laundry, and I was responsible for the balance of the housework and the cooking. Together we attended school programs, of which there were many for several years—three of the four children performed in music concerts every term. I was a super mom of the era.

I loved being assistant to the governor, doing something meaningful for so many people, especially for women and minorities. I felt I was doing what I had been intended to do, carrying out my life mission. At the same time, the combined responsibility of mother and politician was exceptionally challenging. Every couple months, something stressful would occur at work or at home. The combined effort of being a super mom and a public figure would take its toll; I would lose heart.

In my billfold, I carried a quotation from St. Paul in which he remarks that his burden will never be greater than he can bear. Christ had suffered and transcended; with the grace of God, so could I. The problem would gradually resolve; I would take a day or two off, and then throw myself into the maelstrom once again.

Soon after we moved to Olympia, Stan joined the American Legion club where he often spent hours with retired military friends. Utilizing his fine musician skills, he played in their marching band, which practiced once a week at the club. My work in the governor's office was awkward for Stan; clearly, he resented my time away from the family and the children. For his and their sake, I was careful to never schedule more than two evenings away from home in a week. I kept this discipline for eight years.

Aware that I had political responsibilities never before assumed by women, I looked for models, for another woman to mentor me. Finding none in Washington State, I turned to other states and the federal government, seeking married women in politics, but had no success. The search ended one evening as I drove under a railroad overpass near the capitol on my way home from attending a weeknight Mass.

My inner voice telegraphed: *You are the model.*

I cried. Now I understood more about my life mission. God was asking me to become the model. God would give me the strength.

Ten minutes later, I pulled into our driveway, reached for my briefcase, and donned a smile. No point in letting the family see my tears, I thought.

FORTY TO FORTY-FOUR (1972–1976) CABINET DIRECTOR

Shortly after Governor Evans named me the first woman to hold a cabinet position in Washington State government, Ralph Munro, another governor's assistant, placed a picture of a 1912 news photo on the door of my office in the governor's suite. The glossy reprint showed a suffragette leading a parade down New York's crowded Fifth Avenue. A strong wind blew her ankle-length skirt about her striding legs and she carried an American flag that ruffled above her in a strong breeze. The picture was meant to be a joke, but it captured the sense of purpose I had carried since I was eight years old. I left it there to grace the entry to my office until I left state government four years later.

My new political challenges seemed to call forth a deeper spiritual connection; my energy flowed back and forth between politics and spirituality, between my public and private lives. Other women have described a conflict between their feminism and their spirituality. For me, the two worked together to eventually reveal a more authentic self.

Inspired with new faith, I, along with several friends from the Charismatic prayer group, volunteered to help with various parish activities. When the progressive Catholic Archbishop "Dutch" Hunthausen approved the reading of the scripture at Mass by lay people, I was invited to serve. I was delighted. Women were at last being given an opportunity to participate in the liturgy of the church. A year later, in an even more momentous development, I began to distribute Communion. A poem I wrote at the time describes the feeling of awe I had while giving Eucharist to fellow congregants.

The host that heals the world,
The small circumference that encompasses the universe,
God whom I revere and love,
I hold in my hand.
This is the Body of Christ, I say.
They answer, I believe.

I began to hope the changes in the church signaled even more significant change in the future. I hoped that women would be ordained as priests, that even married men and women would consecrate the Eucharist. When several of us were asked to conduct weeknight services—masses in every respect except that we did not consecrate the bread and wine—my calling to ordained ministry deepened.

Over the succeeding four years, my family responsibility began to diminish as the three older children reached high school. As cabinet director for general government, I continued to appoint citizens from all walks of life to both statutory and non-statutory boards and commissions. In addition, the governor often asked me to develop lists of candidates for judicial, cabinet, and departmental positions. Minority and women's rights and affirmative action consumed much of my energy. I met with groups throughout the state, spoke before the legislature, and appeared on radio and television. In addition, I was responsible for a number of key state programs.

Comparable Worth

In early December 1973, a month before the new legislature was to convene, I met with Larry Goodman, lobbyist for the state's Public Employees Union. Across the nation, unions were taking up the cause of equal pay for women. Larry told me, "Even though men and women don't perform the same work, when the skills and educational requirements for their jobs are compared, women are grossly underpaid." He continued, "The union's board of directors wants the governor to include money for a Comparable Worth Study in his new budget."

It was a stunning proposal, one that feminists would enthusiastically support. After I reviewed the request with Jim Dolliver, the governor's executive assistant (later chief justice of the Washington State Supreme Court), a $30,000 line item was included in the preliminary budget. A few days later, the phone on my desk buzzed. I picked up the receiver; Governor Evans was on the line. He said, "Can you come in?"

Grabbing a notebook, I hurried along the twenty-foot corridor separating my office from his suite. Knocking on the door, I entered his spacious office. Seated at his desk, Governor Evans looked up from the page he studied. "What's this?" he asked, pointing to a dollar figure.

"Comparable Worth," I answered. "The union will support a study to find out if women and men are paid equally. The research would determine if it's possible to compare a highway flagman's job to a secretarial position."

"Interesting idea," the governor said slowly. He paused a moment, looked thoughtful, then nodded. "Okay." He grinned at me. "Thanks."

The study legislation was among the first such measures to be proposed and passed in the nation. In retrospect, Comparable Worth became the most consequential issue I handled during my eight years as the governor's assistant. As assistant to the governor and chairwoman of the state's Affirmative Action Committee during the next four years, I oversaw the study and its development.

In two succeeding legislative sessions, Governor Evans requested additional money to complete the study. Our effort culminated in the governor's request in his last budget for millions of dollars to fund implementation of Comparable Worth. Unfortunately, the legislature failed to fund the measure; subsequently, the Public Employees Union sued the state for discrimination, and won. After a protracted series of appeals in federal courts, Comparable Worth eventually died in the United States Supreme Court.

Alternatives for Washington

During his 1972 reelection campaign the year before, Governor Evans had proposed a statewide citizen's goal-setting process, Alternatives for Washington. In 1973, after his successful reelection, I selected more than one hundred fifty citizens, men and women representative of the state's population, then coordinated the three-year program which was to set the tone for Washington State programs for the next twenty years. I attended conferences and worked with staff from the Office of the Budget as well as with the citizen chairman, Reverend Ed Lindemann, president of Whitworth College in Spokane.

On one memorable occasion, a Budget Office staff member and I flew in the governor's plane to Spokane to meet with Reverend Lindemann. On the cross-state flight, we encountered a storm. The four-seat plane bounced around like the proverbial popcorn in a skillet. East of the Cascade Mountains, the pilot dropped down below the thunderclouds to avoid the turbulence, flying low for a hundred miles over rolling green fields of early grain.

Approaching Spokane, our pilot radioed for permission to land. "Okay to land," the cockpit radio crackled, and a few minutes later the plane touched down. As the wheels hit the pavement and taxied toward the state patrol office, another spurt of words came from the tower: "Washington Number One on the ground!"

The First International Women's Day

On another occasion during the tumultuous seventies, I stood near the Great Seal of the state of Washington, at a podium set up on the marble floor under the classic capitol dome. Jennifer Belcher, whom I had hired to help with correspondence two years before (she later ran for office and was elected Washington State's insurance commissioner), and I had arranged for the first International Women's Day rally inside the capitol. A colorful crowd filled the rotunda, the stairs, the balconies above, and spilled out the bronze doors and down the entry steps to groomed lawns. Flags flew, banners waved, and placards proclaimed comparable worth, equal rights for women, and the right to choose.

Magnified a hundred-fold, my voice reverberated through the chambers. To reduce sound distortion, I spoke slowly. "Friends ... we gather ... on this auspicious occasion ... to celebrate women ... to claim rights long denied ..."

Each time I paused, the crowd roared, sharing their hopes and aspirations, willing me on. The sound echoed off the marble, bounced against the walls, and came to rest in the sea of bodies.

Privately, I continued to derive sustenance and support from the Charismatic prayer group. I began to search for evidence of the presence of the Holy Spirit before the birth of Christ. Although the Catholic Church at the time discouraged laypeople from reading the Bible, I read the Old and New Testaments in their entirety. Then, after exhausting the available books on the Charismatic Movement, I began to read Catholic and Protestant mystics. Greatly intrigued, I read about St. Theresa of Avila, later to be named a doctor of the church, and about St. John of the Cross. I dabbled in C. S. Lewis and read about Father Pio, a modern day saint of Italy. Reading mysticism encouraged and deepened my own natural mysticism.

Shortly before the governor's term ended and I left politics, I traveled to the nation's capital on state business. There, ironically from a bookrack in the vestibule of the Catholic National Shrine of the Immaculate Conception, I purchased the book that would lead to my departure from the Roman Catholic Church—a paperback edition of *The Soul Afire, Revelations of the Mystics*.

As I glanced through the book recently, the feeling I had thirty years ago returned. How serendipitous the discovery of the book had been! I had not even heard of synchronicity at the time—now, it seems patently clear that my inner self drew the writing to me, just as my life reached a critical juncture. I would soon leave public office, and my future was clouded.

Most of the compendium, edited by Father H. A. Reinhold, drew from Christian sources, but to my astonishment, the Roman Catholic author included non-Christian writers who emphasized the experience of mysticism. I was searching for transcendence—for union with God. I discovered ecstatic lovers of the divine who provided specific instructions. Meditation, which I had already begun with the Catholic Charismatics, was the key.

FORTY-FOUR TO FORTY-NINE (1977–1982)
TURNING INWARD
Campus Ministry

On the evening of my return with my husband and youngest son from an idyllic three-week camping trip in Baja California, I sat on the deep red carpeted living room floor, my back against the sofa where the children and

I loved to curl up together, reading mail. Finished with the bills and letters, I picked up the archdiocesan newspaper.

Several months before, when I had heard the Vatican was studying the role of women, I had written to the Papal Commission on the Ordination of Women, setting forth the reasons why I felt women should be ordained. While we were out of the country, Pope John Paul II had signed the long-awaited restatement of church policy.

As I read the papal decision to continue the exclusion of women from priesthood, I curled up in the fetal position on the floor and wept, muffling my cries to avoid waking Stan and Greg. Once more, the church had denied the intrinsic worth of women, this time because they did not have the biological makeup of men. John Paul, the young, recently ordained pope, declared that only men could turn bread and wine into the body and blood of Jesus Christ. This, he made clear, was because a man had the physical appearance of Jesus Christ.

In the same time period, since Governor Evans had decided not to run for a fourth term, I no longer had a job and had begun working for work. While I looked for a new position, Lois Parker, director of the Thurston and Mason Counties Alcoholism Center, invited me to conduct a $400,000 capital funds drive for a new treatment facility. This was not a political job; it stemmed out of my prior service as chairwoman of the local United Way Allocations Committee for several years.

One afternoon, some months after I left state government, after meeting with the Olympia Kiwanis club, Lois and I went out to her car to return to the office. As the glass door of the restaurant foyer swung shut behind me, I commented, "Sometimes I think there's a world inside me as large as the one I've worked with in politics. It's probably too late to find out—I'm forty-five."

"What do you mean, another world?" Lois unlocked the car and placed the projector case she carried on the carpeted floor of the trunk.

I unloaded the campaign paraphernalia I had brought. "I'm not sure. Dreams and intuitions, that sort of thing, I guess. Why do we act the way we do? You ever have that feeling?"

As she turned the ignition key, Lois asked, "Have you read Carl Jung?"

I borrowed a copy of *Man and His Symbols* and began to explore my inner world.

A new chapter of my life had begun.

During the fundraising campaign, and for a year after that, I completed several writing and consultant contracts while searching for full-time work. Casting about for what next to do, I contemplated taking a degree in either business or public administration. Both had an accounting prerequisite, so I enrolled in community college to take the classes over the next year. Between consulting assignments, I drew unemployment.

On my job search, I encountered church, community, and social indifference. As my prolonged pursuit of work continued, depression—like winter rain in Washington State—became my constant companion. One morning, I woke from a dream in which I lay in a shallow grave. On another night, I dreamed that I rummaged through clothes racks containing the exact same dress in three different sizes, like the similar jobs I looked for month after month. Putting on and taking off image after image, nothing fit. Depressed over my inability to find a job, I ripped apart a telephone book and wept in frustration.

Failure to find work, as much as spiritual ambition, propelled me inward. Hoping to find my way out of the dark tunnel I had entered, I read Jungian psychology and poured out my feelings in my journal. Reading Eastern and Western mystics, I began to experiment with new forms of meditation. One involved watching my breath; another required the constant repetition of what could be described as a Western mantra, "Lord Jesus Christ, have mercy on me, a poor sinner."

Despite the papal proclamation that prohibited women from priestly ministry, I felt called to help people spiritually. I had completed my political work, but my life mission still beckoned. The Seattle archdiocese, under pioneering Archbishop Hunthausen, newly affirmed women in ministry and instituted several programs involving laity—truly a breath of fresh air in the stagnant old church. For a time after Vatican II—the great convocation of the church under Pope John, I was greatly encouraged. I had been both a lay reader and a Eucharistic Minister for several years. Because of my involvement with the Charismatic prayer group and the ecumenical campus ministry (the year before I left state government, I had become chairperson of the Evergreen State College Campus Ministry), Archbishop Hunthausen invited me to represent the archdiocese on the Washington State Council of Churches. That same year, after receiving archdiocesan training, I began to direct a two-year Parish Renewal Project at our local parish, St. Michael's. Under the liberal archbishop, women in the diocese were doing things not approved by the Vatican.

Unquestionably, the ministry I was conducting in the archdiocese pushed the envelope of the worldwide Catholic Church. But, for me, my involvement always fell short. The pope had declared that women could not be priests. In effect, we could not absolve, marry, bury, or consecrate the bread and wine. We were, in my view and in the view of many other women throughout the country, not equal to men in the church.

In September 1978, Jim Symons, the campus minister at Evergreen, and I traded jobs: he would be the administrator, and I would work on campus as a part-time ecumenical campus minister. Believing the Catholic Campus Ministry office would have ideas about how I might minister on campus, I called to make an appointment with the director of Catholic Campus Ministries in Seattle. We spoke and set a date for me to visit with him. The following week, I drove an hour to his office in Seattle; he was not there when I arrived.

A few minutes later, he entered the room. Looking puzzled, he asked, "Do we have a meeting?"

Extending my hand, I said, "I'm Jo Garceau, the new campus minister at Evergreen. I called last week."

He gingerly shook my hand and quickly moved to a chair behind his desk. Safely ensconced there, he glanced out the window before venturing, "I don't know much about Evergreen. We've never worked with them."

"I know," I replied. He picked up a magazine, flipped through the pages, and placed it back on the blotter. I continued, "The ministry was established only four years ago. St. Mike's Catholic Church in Olympia is one of the nine churches that contribute to the campus ministry budget."

He fidgeted while I related more of Evergreen's history. I said, "I'm looking for ideas and support. Are there classes I could take?"

"I don't know of any."

"What about Seattle University?" A Catholic College, I'd taken a couple classes there.

"No," he paused, apparently thinking, "I don't think so."

"How about reading materials?"

"I can't think of anything," he said. He crossed his legs and leaned back in his swivel chair, then said, "You could always move to San Francisco to attend seminary."

Why is this man, young enough to be my son, so unhelpful? Obviously, he's been taught to distance himself from women; he knows women have no ministerial status in the church, and I don't think he gives a damn. I told him I was married and that I couldn't study in San Francisco. Even if I could, fall quarter was about to begin.

I thanked him for his time and left. As a good Catholic, I had sought validation for my new ministry and come away empty-handed. When I got home, I picked up the phone and dialed Paul McCann, the Presbyterian minister who, with Jim Symons, had started the Campus Ministry. The three of us, all members of the small lunch group that evolved out of the original leadership luncheons committee, were close friends and worked together on the Campus Ministry board.

"Got any idea where I can get some campus ministry training? The archdiocese doesn't have anything."

Paul told me about an external master's degree program offered by the Presbyterian seminary in San Anselmo, California, which would begin the following month in Seattle. Professors from the seminary located just north of San Francisco would teach weekend classes every six weeks for a year; following that, students would complete their degree work at local colleges and universities.

That week, my application, along with four recommendations, went out in the mail. In a few days, I received a phone call accepting me into the program.

Once on a Forest Path

On February 26, 1979, a total solar eclipse occurred in the Northwest United States. Within a few days before or after that rare event, I met a senior at Evergreen College, Garth, whose attentive gaze and generous smile captured my attention. He had a glow about him and seemed more spiritual than anyone I had ever met. At the eclipse, Sun and Moon were conjunct in Pisces by transit and in my house of partnership, trine my natal Sun. In Garth's chart, the solar eclipse lit up his natal Sun. We would often remark in years to come that we felt we had known one another for lifetimes.

A few weeks after our first meeting, we arranged to meet at the Campus Ministry office in the student-housing complex to go for a walk. Garth and I crossed the street from the housing complex and entered a wooded area. We hiked along a deer trail through tall firs, mid-sized vine maples, low salal bushes, and yellow budding Oregon grape. Eventually, I knew the path ended at a sandy beach on quiet Budd Inlet, but as I hiked, I couldn't help wondering where our new friendship would lead.

"You can eat this," Garth said, handing me a furled leaf. The fern tasted green, like the first day of spring. The astringent flavor burst on my tongue, a communion offering from the table of Nature herself. So impressed was I with his love of nature that I wrote a poem to celebrate a new beginning.

> *Once on a forest path*
> *You fed me new life*
> *In a curled, green fern.*
> *I followed you.*

We had not gone far before Garth glanced at his watch and exclaimed, "I'll be late again!" Reversing direction, he headed back along the trail toward the college, his six-foot-four frame covering the ground in long strides. In seconds, he was twenty feet ahead of me. He stopped on a small rise and turned to see if I followed. Silhouetted in light, an aura surrounded him.

My inner voice telegraphed, *Don't let him go out of your life!*

As our friendship grew, Garth told me, "I was twelve when my dad had a heart attack. His death shattered my life. A couple years later, I read about a yoga community in California called Ananda, and Mom agreed to take me there on a visit.

"We stayed a couple days. I was so impressed that I begged Mom to let me attend my last year of high school there."

When Garth completed high school, he had wanted to stay, but did not have a thousand dollars to pay the membership dues, so he returned to Seattle. There, he found a job and earned the money in two months. "I returned to Ananda and became a monk. I've been a member for six years.

"Do you know about Yogananda, the Indian swami who came to the United States in the 1920s?" he asked.

Paramahansa Yogananda

An advanced spiritual master born and educated in India, Paramahansa Yogananda came to the United States in the mid 1920s to teach the science of spirituality. He stated that the West is technologically advanced while the East is spiritually advanced. The world has reached the time for the marriage of the two. See the book *Autobiography of a Yogi* for Yogananda's own story of his life.

"I read his *Autobiography of a Yogi* last fall," I said. "I liked it so much I read it again over Christmas break."

"Swami Kriyananda, the founder of Ananda, is an American who became a disciple of Yogananda right out of college. Master (Paramahansa Yogananda) told Swami Kriyananda his life work is to build World Brotherhood communities," Garth said.

Meeting Garth just after I finished Yogananda's book for the second time seemed to me to be a spirit-guided, synchronous event. Amazed that a monk with a connection to this particular spiritual master had entered my life, I wanted to stay in touch with him.

By the time I had read *Autobiography of a Yogi* for the third time that spring, I had memorized Yogananda's line of teachers. The eternal Babaji, a deathless saint who rarely shows himself, lives in the Indian Himalayas and is the ultimate teacher in the line. During the mid-nineteenth century, while on a trip into the foothills of northern India, Lahiri Mahashaya, a railroad manager, met Babaji and became his disciple. Lahiri had taught Sri Yukteswar, a man of profound detachment and clarity. Yukteswar, in turn, had taught Yogananda before sending him to America in the early 1920s on a mission to bring Eastern meditation and Western technology together.

Fascinated with Garth's knowledge of Eastern spirituality, meditation, and his love of the environment, to satisfy my longing for mystical connection with God, I offered him the campus ministry internship for the following school year. That fall, when he returned from Ananda, he organized a meditation group. Because I thought members of the campus ministry's supporting churches would question Eastern meditation, to alleviate their fears, I arranged to attend the meetings. In truth, after nearly a decade of Charismatic group membership, meditative prayer, and reading Eastern philosophy, I was eager to learn Yogananda's meditation technique.

One evening before the meditation group was to meet for the first time, Garth motioned me into an empty classroom.

"What are we doing?" I asked.

"You wanted to learn to meditate."

"Here? Now?" Rows of student chairs with extended writing arms filled the small room. Outside the half-open window shades, rain fell heavily. Across the way, heavy mist haloed a yellow light, illuminating bare tree limbs. A half-inch of water stood on the concrete path.

"Sure, why not?"

I pulled off my raingear, hat, and gloves and laid them on a desk.

"Sitting with your back straight," Garth instructed, "close your eyes, and focus your attention between your eyebrows. Keep your mind as empty as possible." He said my hands should be loosely folded in my lap; I should be relaxed and attentive. I was to watch my breath, imagining that with every inhalation, energy flowed into my body and rose up my spine, and that, with every exhalation, energy flowed down the spine and emptied out of my body.

I took to meditation like a mother to her first-born child. Practicing daily for increasing lengths of time, behind the endless flow of images and words, I found a steady point of reality. There, no one and no church stood between God and me. Every breath became a Mass; every exhalation, an offering; every inhalation, a gift. My life became an altar.

Healing

My co-minister, Pat McCann, and I had been on the campus for several months before I asked what she thought of hands-on healing.

"I've done it for years," she responded. "I just don't talk about it."

"Me, too," I said. "I'm afraid people will think I'm weird. And I always wonder, who am I to do this? How can I be sure if it helps or hinders?"

That fall, the campus ministry and St. Michael's parish provided the money for a several-month long, hands-on-healing course taught by a Charismatic Catholic priest in Tacoma, a forty-five minute drive away. In his classes, I learned that the Holy Spirit responds to everyone who is receptive, and I gained confidence in the energy that flowed through my hands.

In Yogananda's yoga correspondence course distributed by Self Realization Fellowship, I read about the life force, kundalini, coiled at the base of the human spine until aroused and sent to the head, where it triggers enlightenment. Hinduism defined this divine energy as Shakti, the female consort of the highest god, Shiva. I suspected that Christians knew kundalini/Shakti— the universal, feminine energy—as Holy Spirit/Wisdom/ Sophia, that the energy of Christian healing and the Hindu kundalini were the same.

The I Ching

In the spring of 1980, Garth designed a course on the ancient Chinese oracle, the *I Ching*, also known as The Book of Changes. He asked me to be the faculty advisor, and Evergreen College approved the five-class, one-credit course, which I attended. We used the Wilhelm translation with commentary by C. G. Jung.

For several years after the class ended, I consulted the *I Ching* almost daily. Over time, I found my worldview changing dramatically. In contrast to the static, concrete, rule-based world I had grown up in, the oracle provided a different, now widely accepted philosophical approach: life is never static; change is the norm. One learns to go with the flow. The philosophy of the I Ching fit, too, with the philosophy of relativity that many students had adopted in line with Einstein's theories.

While in the governor's office, I had begun to read astrology. At Evergreen College, a student read my astrological chart for the first time. She knew less of astrology than I did at the time; even so, she was learning to lay out a chart and read, something I had not yet attempted. The reading with Mary piqued my interest and I began to look for a more psychological approach, one that would address the client as an individual interacting with the cosmos, more along the lines of the writing of Dane Rudhyar. My second reading proved to be more satisfying than the first. However, once I had received a psychological reading, I knew that I was searching for a spiritual view, which I eventually found in a devotee of Yogananda whose readings I loved.

As the ecumenical campus minister, I met with students of all faiths, as well as those professing no belief at all. Wanting our ministry to be relevant to students and their concerns, Pat and I listened and supported anyone who sought our help as they experimented with life styles, spirituality, sexuality, and ethics.

One afternoon, a Jewish student wept as she related, "I had an abortion. God will never forgive me."

"Have you asked for forgiveness?"

"No. How can I?"

"Just ask."

"I can't."

I handed her a double-ended crystal about two inches in length and a little less in diameter, called a Herkimer diamond, that I always carried with me. Inside the clear stone was a tiny cavity, a natural feminine space. Using the Jewish word for "the one God whose name cannot be spoken," I suggested, "Why don't we pray to Yahweh?"

Moments later, Leah straightened, brushed away her tears, and smiled.

On another occasion, a student experienced severe abdominal cramps. After she agreed that I could try to relieve the pain, I put one hand on her back and the other on her stomach. She gasped, "Your hands are burning!

"Shall I stop?"

"No." For a moment she seemed to go away, then she exclaimed, "My God! The pain is gone."

The most unusual healing I witnessed involved a scowling, blond science student with horn-rimmed glasses who hung around the campus ministry office. Thinking he wanted to talk, on several occasions I invited him in, but he always declined my invitation. For weeks, he shadowed me, until one afternoon I took the initiative. I sat down beside him on a sofa in the student lounge and handed him the Herkimer diamond.

"What's this?" he demanded.

"A crystal. Double-ended ones like these only grow in Herkimer County, in New York."

"Why'd you give it to me?"

"You're studying geology; I thought it might interest you." He turned the crystal over and over, studying it carefully. In a little while, he began to tell me about a breakup with his girlfriend. He didn't know what to do; sometimes he thought about killing himself. He couldn't ask God for help—he did not believe in him.

"You don't have to name a god to ask for help."

"What do you mean?"

"The universe is full of energy. It creates things, like this Herkimer diamond, and you and me, and all the things you're studying."

"I don't have to talk to him? I can talk to the source?"

I nodded. He beamed. Unfolding his six-foot slender frame, he stood up, bounced the crystal up and down on the palm of his hand a couple of times, and returned it to me. "Gotta go," he said. "I'm late for class."

A few weeks later, he introduced me to his new girlfriend.

I loved being with students on campus, and I enjoyed my master's degree studies—I was reading Piaget, Kohlberg, and others about the stages of human development. James Fowler, who taught religion at a Southern college, had adapted their stage models to faith development. For two years, I met weekly with Jim Symons, Pat McCann, and several others to apply Fowler's theories to our lives and the campus ministry work.

Fowler's faith stages evolve from the child at stage one through a young adult at stage three, whose sense of self is dependent on others. And there most of us stay. A stage four adult recognizes worldviews separate from his or her own and respects these differences. At stage five, an individual freely moves between differing worldviews, returning to his/her choice at will. At still higher stages, the Christ-like individual recognizes all levels as his or her own and demonstrates empathy for everyone. Fowler's theories applied only to Christian faith development. I thought the scheme would apply universally to all spirituality.

Stages of Faith Development

Originally put forth by James Fowler, there are six stages.

Stage One: Primal or Undifferentiated faith
Stage Two: Mythic-Literal
Stage Three: Synthetic-Conventional
Stage Four: Individuative-Reflective
Stage Five: Conjunctive
Stage Six: Universalizing

Because there are seven chakras in the etheric body, I believe there is a seventh stage in which the soul is one with the entirety of creation.

See *Stages of Faith: The Psychology of Human Development and the Quest for Meaning* by James W. Fowler, and *Women's Spirituality: Resources for Christian Development, Joann Wolski Conn (ed), pp 226-232.* See Metaphysics 101 for additional information.

To complete my thesis on the stages of spiritual development, San Anselmo Theological Seminary required that I have a qualified mentor; a friend suggested a member of his church, a prominent Seattle psychotherapist, might be helpful. At a meeting with the therapist in his book-lined office near the University of Washington one afternoon, I said, "Saint Paul writes that now we see dimly as through a glass. What do you think he means?"

"I don't know," he replied. "Why do you ask?"

"An intuition. I suspect a place, a consciousness perhaps, beyond the visible world, from which all creation arises."

"I haven't encountered that," he said.

My search continued for several months until the retiring head of Religious Studies at the University of Puget Sound, Reverend John McGee, agreed to work with me. It was worth waiting. I had never imagined such a memorable and rewarding relationship.

Certain the Christian seminary from which I hoped to graduate and my Roman Catholic and ecumenical peers would label me an outcast for my unorthodox views, I was nervous about the presentation of my theory of universal spiritual development. Now, it is abundantly clear to me that spirituality develops beyond the six stages James Fowler proposed. Rather, the stages of spiritual development relate to the seven chakras—centers of spiritual energy in the human body—and to Carl Jung's theories of the unconscious and the Self. The stages are universal, not limited to a religious belief system.

My meetings with John McGee were delightful, intellectual, and faith-filled. I especially recall one conversation with him. "I cannot reconcile," he said, "your commitment to women's liberation, both in deed and thought, and your description of God as masculine."

"I wish my God were feminine, but he isn't," I said. "Obviously, God is not an anthropomorphic figure with a long gray beard sitting on a cloud making judgments. I've rejected much of the traditional Catholic dogma, and I've devoted years of political effort to improving the status of women, but God remains a male. I doubt my concept of the divine will ever change."

As I practiced the meditation techniques Garth taught me, the energy began to move in my spine, cool currents lifting and falling as I breathed in and out. After a few months, I felt the kundalini energy moving even as I went about my daily activities.

Ananda

"Women lead at Ananda," Asha said. "Seva, our community manager, has been Swami's right hand for years."

Sharon, a friend from the Seattle meditation group, and I had driven to California to attend a five-day women's retreat at Ananda. I was considering moving to the community and wanted to see for myself how residents and Swami Kriyananda viewed women's roles.

As Asha responded to questions, my gaze wandered. Behind us, a dozen tents scattered between tall Ponderosa pine and Douglas fir. A hundred feet beyond the group, to the south, a weathered, brown cabin peeked through bear brush; across the meadow stood a rustic two-story house. In the distance, I could hear a slow-moving truck toiling up the graveled road in low gear. Moments later, the truck passed the level ground on our right and continued up the hill to the retreat buildings.

Asha's voice drew me back. Ending the class with a prayer, she asked us to meet at the office in half an hour. We would be carpooling to the river, taking along a vegetarian picnic supper.

The principal teachers for the week were Asha, a dynamo with a laser mind, iron-willed Shivani, and soft-spoken Anandi, all roughly ten years younger than me. Each day, other Ananda women joined the class; at lunch and dinner during the week, we visited the homes of several community women. Hearing their descriptions of life at Ananda and observing their conduct, I discerned no discrimination. In fact, Ananda women seemed more involved in the community than the men.

Swami Kriyananda had taken a vow of celibacy at his ordination thirty years earlier. That week, while I was attending class, he returned from Hawaii with a beautiful young woman whom he introduced as his wife. Community members appeared to calmly accept the startling news.

On Saturday, Garth and I drove to Sierra Buttes, an hour away. We hiked a half hour up a primitive road, then sat at the edge of Upper Sardine Lake on sun-draped rocks and meditated for the entire afternoon. That night, after a late supper, we threw our sleeping bags down among huge granite boulders. Lying side by side, we talked for hours as the constellations slowly turned overhead. Well after midnight, we said goodnight.

An hour later, an earth movement startled me awake. Deep beneath my pine needle bed, I felt a shifting.

I sat up, exclaiming, "What was that?"

Garth was already on his feet. "I don't know!"

He left me to walk around the area. When he returned, he told me he had not seen anything amiss. "It was probably a small earthquake. Let's go back to sleep."

Although the earth movement was most likely only a localized resettling of the ground under the lake, at the time it seemed an additional evidence of God's activity in my life. It was a deciding moment, a shifting point in time when God spoke to me personally: I should devote my life to Ananda. God was announcing the next step in my lifelong mission to help many people.

I returned home convinced on one level that the community was the answer to my prayers. On a practical level, I was cautious. Even if a picture of Christ occupied the center of every Ananda member's home altar and all community worship areas, clearly the devotion of the community focused on Paramahansa Yogananda. I loved the idea of living in an intentional community where work, play, family living, and prayer were directed toward attaining unity with God. But how could I justify a change of spiritual focus from Catholicism to Hinduism? What would my friends and family say?

Three of my children were young adults, out on their own, finding their way in the world. My husband spent much of his time with his American Legion buddies; he had taken the attitude early on that politics was my affair and limited his public appearances with me. He had always been a Catholic, content to go along with what the church did and asked of members. He questioned my spirituality, but said little about my outside activities.

My parents were retired and traveled a good deal; for the most part, my younger siblings, all involved with their growing families, did not question my spirituality. I imagine they assumed that I was a good Catholic, like them, obedient to the commandments, attending weekly Mass and receiving Communion. Only one sister, involved in a Charismatic Christian prayer group, expressed fear that my path would lead to trouble. She read the *Autobiography of a Yogi* because she loved me and wanted to understand my spiritual direction. But she told me she had nightmares after reading the book, so she taught herself to pray for me in her sleep.

On my return from the Ananda trip, as planned, Stan and I and our youngest son, Greg, left immediately on a camping trip north of Vancouver, Canada, on the eastern shore of the Strait of Georgia. We ferried a river and a bay, and followed a paved road through tree-covered, fjord-like land where green mountain ranges soared vertically up from the blue sea. We set up our tent in a provincial campground near Powell River.

That evening, near the weathered stump of a huge, old growth fir, from which huckleberry bushes and sword ferns grew, in a meditative vision, Christ and Yogananda simultaneously raised their hands and blessed me. Perhaps the apparition was a figment of my imagination; at the time, it seemed a clear validation of my life path, and I acted in concert with it.

That fall, in still another serendipitous event, my husband's workplace offered him an early retirement package, encouraging my hope that he might agree to move to Ananda. In December, five months after I attended the women's retreat, we drove to California. I attended a discipleship ceremony held in the meditation dome at Ananda's old retreat while my husband and son explored Nevada City and the surrounding area.

Since summer, Garth had built a cabin at the monastery. Located on the edge of the mountain, a thousand feet above the north fork of the Yuba River, it offered a spectacular view of pine and madrone-covered ridges stretching thirty miles to the north. When I had tea with him there, he told me, "Swami's decision to bring Parameshwari, the woman he met on his trip to Hawaii last summer, to the community has changed Ananda."

"In what way?" I asked.

"After more than fifteen years of monasticism, Swami is advising us to marry—to become householders. The emphasis is shifting to couples and families."

I could understand my friend's concern; when he had joined the community, he had taken vows of celibacy. Now, he was encouraged to embrace an entirely new way of life. A number of Garth's monk friends had already entered relationships with women in the community.

I, on the other hand, had been married for years. Highlighting marriage and family might be cause for celebration, making it easier for my husband and I to fit into the community. Although I wondered about the impact on individual community members, Kriyananda's change of heart was not a big issue for me. I believed I had found a lifestyle that would bring about the spiritual transcendence I longed for.

After visiting my parents in their desert home near the Mexican border on New Year's Day 1982, Stan, Greg, and I drove home along the spectacular California coast below Big Sur. That day, my husband told me he was impressed with the area around Ananda; he was excited about moving there. He would accept the early retirement package. We made plans to sell our home; I would write my master's thesis and give notice at the campus ministry. Greg, who would graduate from high school in June, said that he would attend the University of Washington that fall. We would tell my parents of the decision later.

One afternoon in the spring of my fourth year on campus, Darrel, my student intern invited me to view videos featuring Jiddu Krishnamurti, the Indian spiritual teacher and mystic. "Sure," I agreed, "let's take a look."

Krishnamurti described individual worldviews as open-ended, discrete entities like geometric structures of various shapes and sizes floating in infinite space. The vastness endured; worldviews—individual selves—came and went. Heady with his concepts after a couple hours of film viewing, to ground my consciousness, I went out beyond the classroom buildings to a meadow where groups of students scattered across the lawn like bouquets of spring flowers.

Lying on my back in the grass, looking up at the cloud-studded sky, I visualized large, open, many-faceted structures floating above me. As I contemplated the blue firmament between the imagined shapes, it occurred to me that this was a metaphor for reality: vast inner space, dotted with shifting points of creation.

Kundalini jolted up my spine. I gasped! Thoughts twirled and twisted; consciousness buckled and reconfigured. In a flash, my sense of self collapsed and reformed. Krishnamurti had been speaking about the non-manifest reality beyond creation that I intuited, the source of all things! My awareness had shifted; not only could one be aware of the manifested form, but conscious also of the vastness of the uncreated, from which all things emerge.

Mystical experiences, for me, are impersonal insights that come with suddenness, not a matter of emotion and feeling. When reading for an astrological client, I describe Uranus as the voice of God, bringing sudden new insights from the celestial plane of awareness. Neptune depicts an expansion of consciousness beyond the mundane, a feeling of oneness, as though one is immersed in a sea of awareness. Both are spiritual and occur in the transpersonal realm of consciousness. Thus, I cannot say that mystical experiences bring joy or happiness, which reflect a personal feeling state. Wonderment is somewhat more descriptive, a sense of being caught up, of being outside one's normal frame of reference.

Years of meditation and inner work would ensue before I recognized spacious background as the Self, the center of my being.

I strolled beside Elliott Bay with Paul Meyer who, since inviting me to the leadership luncheons ten years before, had become my closest friend. "I'm moving to Ananda," I told him. "I want to focus my life on meditation and prayer."

"You've meditated since we met. Why do you need to move?"

"I want to dedicate my life to God. I'd do it as a Catholic, but the church won't ordain me."

"You'd uproot yourself? Leave your family, friends, home, all you've worked for?"

Swallowing tears, I answered, "Something compels me."

When one studies my astrological chart in light of the transits of the planets occurring in late July 1982, just before my husband and I moved to a single, wide mobile home near Ananda, the "something" compelling me then seems vividly clear. The year before, Saturn had joined the transformational planet, Pluto, in my second house of values, grounding my spirituality in a new way. In the summer, Mars, the planet of action, had joined these two planets of change.

More dramatically, Uranus, the planet of change and celestial inspiration, had been hovering near the foundation of my chart, the nadir, bringing new soul level insights. These were due to continue another several years. Neptune, the sign of expansive consciousness, was in the house of my home; what better sign that I would make my home in a spiritual community?

And finally, Chiron, the wounded healer, a planet that slowly moves around the sky, returning to its natal position in fifty years, was atop its natal position in Taurus. Situated at the top of my chart, Chiron worked on healing the major hurt of my lifetime, the limitation I felt from patriarchal church and society.

We had shared our decision to move from Olympia with my extended family, many of whom questioned the move itself to an intentional community. Stan and I would continue attending Catholic Church in California, so that was never an issue. Our grown children were busy in their new lives and accepting of the change. Only Greg expressed concern; he would be going away to college in the fall and would be a long way distant. However, he knew he had a home with us wherever we settled.

Spiritual Community

FORTY-NINE TO FIFTY-FOUR (1982–1986)
ANANDA
A Dinner Plate Heart

We scheduled our arrival for Spiritual Renewal Week, Ananda's annual August retreat. The highlight of the year, Swami Kriyananda taught classes every morning under the trees; in the afternoon, devotees from around the country and residents meditated, swam in the Yuba River, and enjoyed picnic suppers. For the gala Indian banquet on Friday evening, everyone painted spiritual symbols on their foreheads, women dressed in colorful silk saris, and men wore white dhotis. Guests and members dined by candlelight under the stars, while sitar music played.

To ease my introduction into the community, I had arranged to take a two-week, live-in leadership class at the meditation retreat immediately after Spiritual Renewal Week. Since I hoped to become a leader at Ananda, the class seemed a fitting beginning for my new life.

One afternoon, as the group discussed power in relationships, I remarked, "I intimidate people. To empower them, I deliberately put myself below others."

"What do you mean?" Asha asked.

"People expect me to lead. If I get out of the way, they take responsibility." I mentioned the Parish Renewal project in Olympia that I had directed before coming to the community. "Everyone waited to be told what to do. Instead of making decisions, I sat on the floor, so those above me would feel empowered."

"You'll never be happy," Asha said, "until you own your power."

That evening, when I arrived at her home for dinner, she had piled cushions on a chair. She invited me to sit on the makeshift throne above the other guests. So embarrassed, I barely avoided crying. At the time, I could not fathom what spiritual lesson she meant to convey.

Twenty-five years after that embarrassing moment, I think Asha knew that to claim my power, I would have to relinquish dependence on external approval. I would need to live from the center of my being. When I arrived at Ananda, I believed I was there to find God; in fact, I was beginning a search for my true Self, the god/goddess within.

In the leadership class, we discussed mantras—the repetition of holy sounds and words to focus thoughts on the divine. *Om Mani Padme Hum,* the famous Tibetan mantra, is one example; another is the simple Catholic mantra I learned as a child and used to say to release souls from purgatory— *Jesus, Mary, Joseph.* Still another, practiced by Russian Orthodox Christians, *Lord Jesus Christ, have mercy on me, a poor sinner,* is acclaimed by many for its power to heal all manner of things. Asha told us *Om* was the highest mantra, signifying that moment when sound first arises out of silence, out of the creative potential. Ramakrishna, an Indian master and contemporary of Paramahansa Yogananda, whom I would not discover for another year, said Om is God, but I did not know that then. Why, I wondered, would anyone choose a lesser mantra? If Om was ultimate, it was my choice.

As in any setting, at Ananda, life was mixed with light and darkness, sadness and joy. Severing all connection with my former life and devoting myself to spiritual practice, my prayer became, *"My body, mind, and soul come from thee, oh God, and unto thee I dedicate them."*

At times, I was supremely happy, certain I had arrived where God intended me to be; most days, however, fitting into the community required perseverance and unwavering determination. Wanting to fit in, wanting to establish my role in the community's worldwide spiritual mission, I volunteered full time. Two months after my arrival, Asha's husband, David Praver, offered me a position in the Ananda Spiritual Family, the community's outreach office that stayed in touch with devotees around the world. For the next year, I wrote letters to devotees, helped publish a monthly newsletter, and conducted healing prayers for far-flung members of the organization.

Three hundred sixty-five days a year, we rolled out the proverbial red carpet for guests—decorating, cooking fine vegetarian cuisine, playing music, and singing Kriyananda's songs. Whenever he was home—Kriyananda traveled frequently to India and Europe—Swami read a new play or an excerpt from his latest book, played a musical piece, or delivered a new insight in class or at Sunday service.

At my weekly postulant class, one evening, Mary asked, "Why are we always trying something new? Wouldn't it be better to give a business a good try for several years?"

"Can't we figure out what grows well on this soil? Maybe, then, we would show a profit," John chimed in.

"We're a pilot community. If one plan doesn't succeed, we try another," a long-time community leader explained. If we don't like the way something's going, we try something else."

Each postulant was encouraged to choose a spiritual director from among the long-time community members. My first spiritual director, Shivani, a fiery devotee with a keen focused mind, whom I admired tremendously, left within a few months after my arrival. Swami Kriyananda had asked her to start a community in Italy—an enterprise that has been eminently successful. Later, Seva, the long-time community manager, and Asha, minister at Ananda's Palo Alto church, were my spiritual directors.

One of the woman ministers I talked with in the first weeks after my arrival at Ananda told me, "You've been a leader. Now, your spiritual task is to learn to follow." I had moved to Ananda because I felt impelled to help with the community's worldwide spiritual mission, and until then, I had never failed to accomplish what I set out to do. Her words only encouraged me to work harder. Given enough time, I was sure that I would succeed.

Lacking close friendships, I concentrated on spiritual practice, practicing mantras as I worked and meditating morning and evening. In my daily meditations, I focused on loneliness, experimenting to see how long the feeling would last—and made a significant breakthrough: emotion was ephemeral! I could not hold my mind on a single thought. Like a chimp moving from tree branch to tree branch, my consciousness jumped from idea to idea, from feeling to feeling.

Instructors in Eastern meditation often focus on "monkey mind"—the idea that the mind is restless, always seeking new entertainment—saying that when one tames the monkey and becomes centered in the emptiness between thoughts, one truly meditates. That emptiness between thoughts reminded me of the spacious sky between Krishnamurti's constructed worldviews. As I focused on emptiness, as I let thoughts go, I found myself spending more and more time in blissful silence.

After a year in the Spiritual Family office, I accepted a bookkeeping position. Over the next two and a half years, I learned to apply the accounting theory I had studied after leaving the governor's office to Ananda's numerous profit and non-profit businesses.

During the several years I worked in accounting, twice a week when Swami was in residence, I attended his lectures where yogic principles were applied to every aspect of life. Trusting the words would sink into my unconscious where they would be available when I needed them, I trained myself to listen from a diffused state of consciousness, aware and floating free. I wanted to feel Swami Kriyananda's spiritually high energy, and to match my energy to his. In time, I learned to maintain a state of inner quiet for hours, sometimes for whole days.

Some Yogic Practices

- Do not be attached.
- Give all to God.
- Attune to the guru.
- Meditate.
- Be open to guidance.
- Let go of the ego.
- Be supple, free, and joyful.

As I practiced meditation, kundalini activated more strongly. Asking ministers about the coolness I felt in my spine, I was told, "It's natural; don't pay attention to it. Focus on God and the gurus." Or, "Don't become sidetracked in phenomena; keep your focus on the third eye, the point between the eyebrows."

The rush of energy was wonderful, and the advice was excellent.

At Ananda, I was outwardly joyous—yet, for days and then months, I carried a pain the size of a dinner plate in the center of my chest. The more successful my spiritual practice became, the more the ache—the opening of the heart chakra—nagged me. Meditation exacerbated my underlying malaise, first experienced growing up Catholic, and then later as a woman in patriarchal society. The more I meditated, the more aware I became of my unhappiness. Meditation, worship services, chanting, yoga postures, Swami's classes, and long hours of work deadened the pain. Escaping into transcendent bliss became my goal. I became an expert, gradually increasing my sitting time to three hours a day.

After not having seen Garth privately for months, on an early spring evening, he and I drove to the river. Parked under a leafing tree, we talked.

"I've been in denial all my life," I told him.

"That's hard to believe," he replied. "You always seem to know what you want."

"I can handle most things," I agreed. "But I'm beginning to see that I've kept myself busy all my life to escape my inner pain. Most of my life has been an escape. I volunteer. I eat. I read myself to sleep. I run away from my feelings—I don't even acknowledge they exist. I've pretended all my life—denied things I couldn't endure. Now, when I wake up in the morning, my heart aches."

Garth rolled down the car window and leaned out to look up at the night sky. I continued, "It's all avoidance. I'm afraid of what's hidden underneath. I've always been afraid, but I've kept it so hidden, even I didn't know."

Garth chided, "You're thinking too much."

Free at Last

"Do you love him?" Asha asked.

I had sought counsel about my deteriorating marriage. "We've been married more than thirty years. He's the father of my children."

"Staying in a marriage can be a spiritual path," Asha commented.

"Yes," I agreed, wiping my nose. "But this doesn't feel spiritual. We don't have the same interests. All he does is read war stories and listen to the news to find out who died. He has never felt adequate. He resents everything I do."

"Why don't you leave him?"

"He says I should." My voice cracked. "I asked God, What about the children? What will my family think? What am I supposed to do? I don't want to disrupt our lives."

Soon after I spoke with Asha, Stan and I agreed to separate as soon as he found work and could move. At Christmas, my husband confided in our son Warren, who was twenty-five, and our son Gregory, who was eighteen; I talked with our oldest son, Paul, and our daughter, Suzanne, who had married four years before and was working in Seattle. Except for Greg, the children approved. My daughter told me, "Save your money; my husband and I'll take you to India."

I waited for Stan to find work; I wanted him to be the one who actually took the deciding step to end the marriage, not me. Half a year later, on Memorial Day weekend, still waiting for a new job for him, we drove to Yosemite National Park. On the last evening, in a camp on the bank of a chattering mountain stream fifty miles south of Lake Tahoe, I meditated.

Later, as I lay in my sleeping bag looking up at the stars, thinking about our years together, a meteor streaked across the sky. Remembering the one we saw the night before our wedding, after months of hesitancy, I made the final decision to leave Stan. *A shooting star began our marriage; another ends it. I'll take the responsibility; I'll leave him.* My marriage of thirty-two years was at an end.

Astrologically, Saturn had been in my third house of everyday affairs and communication for two years, and Pluto had recently joined him there. The two of them were calling for a complete revision to my way of communicating. Emphasizing the importance of communication and doing the work for which I was intended, four planets were in my tenth house, which happens to be Gemini, not surprisingly the house of communication. The four planets in my tenth house were Mars (the planet of action), Sun, Chiron (the planet of healing), and Mercury (the planet of communication). Mercury is the only archetypal energy capable of traveling in all levels of consciousness—underworld, everyday affairs, and celestial; this alone could have been signaling work to be done in guiding souls.

On our way home the following day, we followed highways that crossed two nine-thousand-foot passes and then dropped down to Lake Tahoe. As we drove along the western shore of the pristine blue lake, joy surged through me. The entire country glowed. Trees were alight. Bushes shimmered. The lake glistened. My heart sang. Focused on the glory around and in me, I watched as mile after mile passed. For nearly two hours, the uplifted mood continued, dissipating only after we left the lakeshore.

Two months later, during the August 1985 Spiritual Renewal Week, I waited dinner tables at The Expanding Light. Afterward, I left the social activities and climbed to a spot overlooking Ananda village. Shaded from the late setting sun, I sat under a pine tree in tall, yellow grass. Around me, gnats, mosquitoes, and no-see-ums buzzed. I began to meditate.

Soon, I felt myself soar out beyond the treetops, beyond the thin, hot-weather clouds, out, out beyond the sun, beyond the planets. I kept going—beyond galaxies and star systems—until I floated free in star-spangled black velvet, so far beyond Earth it seemed I could not return. I felt myself alone in the cosmos, a tiny speck in all time; my breath caught; I gasped. The sheer thinness of line between the edge of the universe and myself shocked me, and I cried. *I chose this freedom, this vastness. I want God—God is here in this silence. Yes, God is with me.* Yet I knew my vision was only a mental deception. With a shift of my body, I was back with the pain, back with my aching dinner plate heart.

The following afternoon, I was dusting furniture at The Expanding Light when another Ananda resident working in the kitchen called my name. I answered. A lone guest reading in a quiet corner looked up, startled. "Are you Jo? Jo Garceau? I've been looking for you all week! I'm Susan from Guerneville. Do you remember calling us last April?"

I nodded. I had called to ask for a contribution for the building fund and tried back several times later without success. *Why is she so animated?*

"I couldn't talk because our daughter had something in her throat. You said you'd pray for her and call back."

"I remember."

Her words tumbled out, "Lisa was turning blue. We thought she was dying! After you hung up, she choked up the food and her breathing eased. It was a miracle! A real miracle. We're so grateful. I wanted to thank you."

I was a member of the Healing Prayer Committee and often prayed for people at a distance. I knew the power of prayer even at many miles distant. Of course, I knew I was not the doer, but simply a channel for divine energy—still it was lovely to hear of such blessings.

"Don't thank me," I said. "I just prayed. Thank God."

We talked a little before I left her and went out on the deck surrounding the retreat center. Above the tree line, a double rainbow arched across the late summer sky. What a wonderful affirmation, I thought. I had been lonely for weeks, but God seemed to be saying I would be fine. Not to worry.

Months passed. At the Old Retreat, the original Ananda land located five miles up the North San Juan ridge from the main community, I moved into the rustic, one-room cabin at the edge of the meadow where I had camped on my first visit to Ananda.

Lying in bed one night, I heard a murmuring, like ocean waves lapping on the shore. I imagined the sound came from the wind in the Ponderosa pines. For weeks, I wondered why I sometimes heard the throbbing and sometimes did not. Then, on a still night when no breeze stirred, under brilliant stars in an ebony sky, I recognized the sound: Om!

That October, instead of taking me to India, my daughter, Suzanne, and son-in-law, David, moved from Seattle to the Old Retreat and converted the blue office dome into a home. There, on December 14, during an early snowstorm, Shanti, my first grandson, was born.

Once a week, I went to Grass Valley eighteen miles away to buy groceries and do my laundry. Occasionally, I went to the mountains, to the river, to another city. One weekend, I drove two hundred miles to Mount Lassen to bask in the exhilarating view from a scenic pullout ten thousand feet up the mountain. Reluctant to return and afraid to stay alone in a tent, I slept in my locked car.

The following year, in 1985, growing more confident, I purchased a lightweight backpacking tent, a down sleeping bag and pad, and a single-burner stove, and began to venture out on longer trips. Eventually, I spent a week camping along the California coast, visiting Yogananda's homes in Los Angeles and Encinitas and his crypt at Forest Lawn cemetery.

When the community sponsored its first Holy Land pilgrimage—three weeks in Israel and a week in Italy, an Ananda Spiritual Family member wrote from her winter home in San Miguel, Mexico, "I would love to travel with you."

I wrote back, "Rennie, I'd love to go, but I can't afford the trip."

She phoned and said, "I just received an inheritance, enough to pay for both of us. Please come with me."

Before our October departure, I sold the mobile home my husband and I had purchased when we moved to the community three years before; happily, I said good-bye to the last reminder of my failed marriage. In a remarkable congruence of events, on that same day, my position in accounting ended and I signed divorce papers. Flying east with fifty other pilgrims, I exulted, "No husband, no job, no home! I'm free!"

In the sky, the destiny points, the north and south nodes, were challenged by Jupiter, planet of the spiritual teacher. Moon joined the north node in Taurus, and Sun and Pluto, planet of death and rebirth, were at the south node. Especially significant, Saturn and Mercury were also in Scorpio; a five-symbol powerhouse had formed in the sign of death and rebirth, all triggered by the planet of the spiritual guru, Jupiter in Aquarius. Calculating the midpoint of the five energies in Scorpio, stunningly they met exactly over my natal Sun. A more surprising confluence of energies could not be imagined.

Brilliant Light, Blinding Light

The pilgrimage to Israel and Italy confirmed everything I had learned as a child about Catholicism. Whether in the United States, Israel, or Italy, Catholicism is much the same; I imagine it is wherever one goes. Churches in all three countries had the same incense smell, the same liturgies, the same statues and ambience.

We began and ended our three-week visit in Jerusalem. At the first church we visited in the Old City, the Church of St. Anne, mother of the Virgin Mary, I felt as though I were back in St. Edward's Church in North Plains, Oregon, still four years old. The difference was that this church had been standing for centuries.

After a day or two to rest and orient, our group of fifty pilgrims left Jerusalem to travel around the small country, which is barely two hundred fifty miles long and one hundred miles wide. We stopped first at Megido, the prophesied place of Armageddon. There, while Israeli jets scrambled overhead, we stood atop the tell—the archaeological dig located on the site of the ancient city—chanting for peace. The country is too short for a long jet flight; chasing Syrian jets that had encroached on Israeli airspace, the fighter planes screamed overhead, making an abrupt vertical climb to avoid going into another country, filling the air with sonic booms. It was frightening; the harmonic sounds of the group chanting Om over and over helped to allay my fear, but were far from completely settling.

Inside the modern church at Mount Tabor, built atop ruins of a sanctuary erected by crusaders in AD 700, we meditated. Afterward, as I wandered the grounds, I spotted a keystone in a falling down abutment to the old church; holding it in my two hands, I admired the chiseled form. I imagined that a stocky, tunic-clad man with short hair had shaped the rough-hewn stone thirteen hundred years before. How immediate he seemed!

On the tour, we began every morning with an hour meditation, sometimes alone and sometimes together. For weeks before we left Ananda, we had practiced Swami Kriyananda's libretto, "Christ Lives in the Holy Land and in You." The music was beautiful; the sound of our voices filled chapel after chapel as we traveled from one end of the country to the other.

In the narrow river Jordan, when we entered the stream and were baptized by immersion, I felt wet but experienced no epiphanies; the lovely and simultaneously curious ceremony echoed my baptism as an infant, but was not especially inspiring.

We stayed in a kibbutz, a modern Jewish settlement I had been curious to see, east of the Sea of Galilee; we waded in the lake and climbed the hill where Jesus had delivered the Sermon on the Mount. I tried to wrap my mind around the thought that individuals like myself had lived here two thousand years before; the foundations of an ancient religious institution were established at these locations. When Christ lived, none of his contemporaries would have imagined the beginning of a world religion. He was a simple rabbi, son of ordinary people like me. He had not been well respected in his hometown.

I sat meditating a long time in the hot, early afternoon sun near the front of the ancient temple where Jesus was said to have preached. I imagined him standing before the congregation, speaking. The vibration of the place was powerful and holy, and there I especially felt the incredible, steel-like determination that Christ had—to do his father's will, no matter the outcome. I was determined to be as strong in my faith as he had been in his.

I remember especially a personal meditation on the lawn outside the kibbutz, beginning at daylight and lasting well into midmorning. In the distance below, the Sea of Galilee glistened in the bright sunshine; behind me, a barricaded air raid shelter occupied the side of the hill. How remarkable it was to be in Israel—the site of conflict for millennia—sitting in absolute, unlimited silence and feeling my awareness expand into infinity. In the meditation, I reached a state of utter stillness in unconditioned emptiness. In itself, the meditation was like every sitting, a complete absence of thought, time suspended. However, to be able to sit in this particular site, feel the warmth of the sun on my shoulders, hear the birds in the nearby bushes, see the rippling, wind-directed currents on the water, was unique in my experience. Nothing changed, and that was the beauty of it; Christ, or any man or woman who sat there two thousand years before, might have had the exact same experience.

After visiting Nazareth, we traveled south on the western side of the Sea of Galilee to the ancient city of Jericho, then to the Dead Sea where we immersed ourselves among salt pillars. While not spiritually inspiring, it was curious and memorable. The mineral-filled water was unusually buoyant. When we learned to balance ourselves, we walked out some distance among the pillars and felt the smoothness of the water on our lower limbs.

On the return north to Jerusalem, we stopped at Qumran. After meditating, I climbed over and around stone walls at the ancient Essene community site immediately above the cave where the Dead Sea Scrolls had been found hidden in a pottery jar.

Upon our arrival in Israel, I had asked about visiting the Eastern Orthodox Church of Mary Magdalene; our guide had told us the church was closed to outsiders. Still, as we traveled the country, I often thought about Mary Magdalene. I continued to hope we might visit the church when we returned to Jerusalem.

One morning after our return from the Dead Sea, we visited the Church of Gethsemane at the Garden of Olives where Christ prayed before being taken into Roman custody. We had sung only a song or two when we were asked to stop. To our surprise, twenty-seven Polish priests and a cardinal concelebrated Mass. I had grown up knowing of the suppression of the Polish Church during the Russian occupation. For years, the church had prayed for their freedom. It was an especially poignant moment to be with them in Jerusalem and to receive Communion that day.

We had just left the Church of Gethsemane when a Russian-speaking Ananda member came running toward us from the street above. Breathless from his run, he told us he had obtained permission for us to visit the Church of Mary Magdalene a couple blocks up the hill. My prayer had been answered; we were able to enter the sanctuary of Christ's saintly consort and experience her peace and holiness.

On another day, we visited the Dome of The Rock, one of the holiest places in the world, revered by Christians, Jews, and Muslims. A blessed place, the cavernous interior vibrated with the devotion of millions over centuries. The spectacular, ornately tiled dome rose one hundred feet above the floor. At its highest point, in the center, was a small hole, perhaps four or five inches in diameter.

To look up through this aperture, we entered a small room below the level of the main floor. The little room was crowded with impatient people who pushed and jostled one another. I did not feel safe. Hostility was palpable. We were light skinned; to the curious Muslim, we were probably Christian or Jewish, and not welcome. Everywhere in the Old City, Israeli soldiers with guns guarded the entries; at best, our presence was tolerated.

But at the Dome of the Rock, gazing up at the exquisitely decorated, curved ceiling, jostled by strangers, a remarkable thing happened. As I looked up, my mind filled with light. Thought disappeared.

The next day, a Muslim holiday, a friend and I were caught in the Old City between uniformed Israeli children and a phalanx of angry Muslims. Tempers were high. Suddenly, we were at the periphery of a riot waiting to explode. My friend and I held hands to avoid being separated in the melee and raced to safety.

The most unusual experience in Israel occurred the day we walked the Via Dolorosa, the path Christ followed to the cross. At the hotel that morning, I woke to light. Brilliant light. Blinding light. Rennie, my companion, said it seemed normal to her, but for me the light was overwhelming. Even with the shades pulled, much more light than was comfortable flooded the room. My eyes watered and I squinted to dim the brightness.

When Rennie and I entered the hotel lobby to meet the other pilgrimage members, the light from outside was even more intense. Another friend, Nancy, noticed my discomfort. I explained that the light was so bright I could hardly bear to open my eyes. She found a pair of wrap-around ski glasses for me. On the bus, even when I wore the glasses, too much light came through.

We entered the Old City by an eastern gate. On the way, we would stop at a small shrine to meditate and sing, before proceeding along cobblestone paths to the Church of the Holy Sepulcher. Keeping my eyes closed, I held Nancy's hand as we walked a quarter mile from the bus to the chapel. Too upset and distracted to meditate, I sat outside in the shaded chapel courtyard and attempted to calm myself. Gradually, my eyes adjusted and I could see again.

I never found an explanation for the brilliance I experienced. It could have been a spiritual phenomenon, or perhaps the dry air and the dusty environment irritated my eyes. The experience occurred only once—on the day we walked the Via Dolorosa.

We continued along the route to the Church of the Holy Sepulcher, entering the building from above. Of the six Christian sects who claim ownership of the holy site, the Coptics have a space on the roof, atop the main church. We literally walked on the flat roof of the church, threading our way along a narrow pathway that wound between tiny beehive shaped domes, each housing a single monk, perhaps as many as twenty or twenty-five separate living spaces.

Passing through a low door, we entered a corridor along the interior of the Coptic Church, approximately thirty by thirty feet in its entirety. Wooden doors enclosed the sanctuary, hiding the altar and the holy of holies from curious bystanders and worshippers. In the center aisle, between the rows of pews, stood a small, dark-skinned priest displaying a hand-printed and illuminated Bible in the shape of a cross. He slowly turned, his arms uplifted, making sure everyone had the opportunity to view the Holy Bible. White light filled my mind. Thought temporarily departed; it seemed a brief cessation of ordinary reality, a blessed radiance that affirmed the sacredness of the artifact we viewed.

After our stay in Israel, the group visited Assisi, Italy, home of two of the holiest saints of all Christendom, St. Francis and St. Clare. Renewed in spirit, we returned to Ananda.

The Yurt

The minister at Ocean Song, an Ananda-operated property on the Northern California coast, had invited me to help her develop a guesthouse and retreat center. After I returned from Israel, my daughter, two-year-old grandson, and I drove over to see the spectacular property, located on rolling hills a mile from the ocean. Pleased with what I found and eager for a ministerial opportunity, I prepared to move.

The day before I was to leave, the Ocean Song minister phoned. "I'm sorry, Jo," she said, "Don't come. Swami Kriyananda has decided to return the property to the owner."

I scrambled to find a place to live—a guest cabin at the Old Retreat—and a job, writing publicity for The Expanding Light. A few weeks later, a yurt on the hill above the dairy became available and I drove over to see it.

Parking my car at the end of the road, I followed a deer trail up a steep hill through trees and small bushes. Turning a bend, I saw a small, round structure nestled against the hill one hundred feet above me. On its lower side, peeled poles supported the canvas building; on the upper side, a three-foot porch fit the curve of the land. Modeled after the homes of Siberian nomads, the yurt was twelve feet in diameter with a dome roof; crisscrossed, two-inch lathes framed the interior fabric walls.

Inside, under the window and next to the sink, a two-burner Coleman stove sat atop a small storage cabinet. Kerosene fueled the lights and space heater; when the temperature rose above freezing, I would have cold water from a hose outside. I moved in immediately.

I slept under cozy blankets on a four-inch foam pad laid out on the varnished, yellow pine floor. On clear nights, stars filled the sky; deer foraged outside, so close—and the canvas walls so thin—I could hear them chewing. One evening as I drifted off to sleep, a doe and a yearling grazed nearby. An owl hooted a quarter mile away, startling the deer; the ground vibrated under their hooves as they ran, setting up a resonance I felt in my half-sleep.

One week out of four, the full moon shone through the un-curtained windows. Soft shadows spread across the polished floor. Month by month, I moved my pad and blankets, following the moon south and west. Old books warned of moon madness if the full moon shone on one, but I knew differently. With the full moon came a fullness of being—an intuitive knowing beyond rational thought, identification with the heart of nature.

As the weather warmed, I bundled up and meditated entire mornings on the sheltered north porch. Birds flew in and joined me, then moved on with a tiny flutter. At the porch edge, three-inch long, leathery green salamanders stretched, absorbing the heat of the late winter sun. One morning, I felt a stir of air, a tiny vibration near my cheek. Carefully, slowly, I lifted an eyelid to see what was causing it. A yellow and gray hummingbird with speckled throat feathers hovered at my mouth, its beak dipping for moisture between my open lips.

Meditating, reading, and writing, I built a castle of silent joy, a hermitage of the heart. Alone, I enjoyed a kind of global immersion. Peaceful and serene, I resisted going out, knowing my unity would be shattered. Leaving the yurt broke my connectedness with God, with the land, with deep silence.

In sharp contrast, when I was with others, I experienced a loss of self. I became the zeitgeist of the moment for as long as the connection—with a friend, family member, or guest—lasted. Relating to others for hours while I was with them, I was unaware that my energy was draining away. Leaving them, I experienced our separation as a great loss, accompanied by overwhelming sadness.

Both conditions—being with others or alone—satisfied me; however, the transition from one state to the other caused emotional devastation. I had experienced this loss all my life without knowing why. For many years, busyness had covered the hole in my heart; now, the emptiness seemed related to my habitual denial of self.

Each time I went out, I coached myself: this time, this time, I'll feel at home among my spiritual friends. But it never worked. When I was with other devotees, I pretended, as I had always done. Anandans told me I looked sublimely happy; guests called me Joy. Like a small white hand in a soft leather glove, I acted as if I belonged in the community while my heart's perpetual turmoil threatened my self-control. Life seesawed between the truth I perceived and the reality others appeared to live. My fragile self swung back and forth, a pendulum pointing first to my knowledge, then to

Ananda's truth, oscillating between awareness of my duplicity and my need to be accepted. If only I could be like them, I thought, I would be at peace.

The problem lay in me: because I had not found my true Self, like many, perhaps most women and men, I externalized my value—if they loved me, I would be happy.

At Easter, I waited tables at a wedding banquet. As usual, pretending joy I did not feel, I observed the festivities from the sidelines. ("Smile!" my grandmother had instructed when I was nine. "If you don't smile, people will think you're angry." Taught from an early age to always appear happy, at the end of a long day in the governor's office, my face had sometimes ached from smiling. By the time I arrived at Ananda, I had a perfect false smile.) As soon as I could leave without being noticed, I slipped away. Crossing the greening meadow, I entered the woods above the village. Safely hidden, I began to cry.

Ten minutes later, as I neared the dairy, a car approached on the road behind me. Swami Kriyananda and Rosanna—the beautiful, young Italian woman he had married the previous summer—were returning to the Hermitage. They stopped to offer me a ride. Suppressing my inner tumult, I smiled a greeting.

"How are you?" Swami asked.

A God-given opportunity for spiritual guidance, I thought. Nothing ventured, nothing gained.

"Fine!" I answered cheerfully, "Although it's not easy being a single, older woman in gatherings like the one we just left."

"What do you mean?" Rosanna asked.

"With people or alone, I'm happy; moving from seclusion to being with people, or reversing the process—from the group back into seclusion—is hard. Swamiji, do you ever experience that?"

"I can't say that I do," Swami answered.

At the turnoff to the yurt, I jumped nimbly out of the car, wished them a joyful Easter, and waved as they drove away.

A few steps up the trail, I sobbed aloud.

Assistant Center Leader

Memory suggests that I was meditating with salamanders on the porch of the yurt, and in the next instant, I was perched on the edge of a chair using a Macintosh computer to create a center newsletter. Quite suddenly, I replaced a couple returning to Ananda's main community and became assistant leader of the San Francisco Center. It was a heaven-sent opportunity, the ministry assignment I had worked toward for four years.

Fortunate to have a room of my own in the huge, old mansion overlooking San Francisco's marina that served as a community residence, I moved into a small room previously occupied by a four-year-old child under the stairs on the second floor. The maid's quarters when the house was built at the turn of the twentieth century, the room was just wide enough for a single bed. A tiny closet hid beneath the steps to the top floor, and a small window overlooked the side entrance to the back porch.

My duties included teaching meditation, conducting classes, and counseling residents during the week. On Sundays, with Rick, the center leader, and other residents, I purchased altar flowers, set up a rented room in the Marina district for church services, and after service, visited over coffee and bagels with center members. In addition, I wrote the monthly center newsletter.

On a typical weekday, I joined other residents in the basement temple for early morning and late evening meditations. Seated on prayer benches, legs tucked under narrow boards, or cross-legged on pillows, we chanted, practiced breathing techniques, and meditated. Used for years for daily practice, a powerful, vibrational resonance had built up in the temple. I spent hours there; often my consciousness floated on a sea of white light, aware at a remote level of ships passing under the Golden Gate Bridge, sounding foghorns breaking the deep silence like some distant siren's call announcing a dangerous reef.

With Rick and Gary, a long-time resident at the center, I shared the weekly grocery buying, purchasing fruits and vegetables in bulk at a greengrocer's near the ocean several miles away. In the market, I slipped into an artist's palette of red, green, orange, and purple produce, choosing the peak of the crop, tasting exotic foods, and inhaling tantalizing fragrances. On my way home, I stopped in Haight-Ashbury to pick up grains, herbs, and spices at an organic grocery. My car overflowing, I returned to the center where residents helped unpack and store the bounty I brought.

A few weeks after my arrival, Rennie, whom I had accompanied on the tour to Israel, called about the upcoming India pilgrimage. Could I go with her? She would provide the balance of my fare, if I could come up with a thousand dollars. It was another rare opportunity to travel, and for the next three months, I worked housecleaning jobs around the city to save money for the trip.

During the week before our departure, I went to Point Reyes National Seashore, twenty-five miles north of San Francisco. After driving in a steady rain to the lighthouse on the south end of the peninsula, I reversed direction and drove to the north end. As I paralleled the coastline, a thin line of light developed on the horizon where cloud and sea met. Would I see a sunset? Not likely, I supposed.

As my car crested the hill overlooking the tip of the peninsula, the herd of Tule elk that frequents the remote reaches of the peninsula came into view, scattered in groups of three or four across the rolling green hills. Overhead, bands of red-gold lit the entire sky, an extravagance of color from horizon to horizon. Everywhere I looked—north, west, south, and east—the sky lit up with shades of orange and red and pink. I was the only one there for miles in any direction to see the beautiful display.

For some time, I sat contemplating my future. Perhaps my usual state of being, like rain and clouds, would lift and I would experience internal glory as brilliant as the splendor before me. The trip to India seemed blessed, and life in the San Francisco ashram was busy and exhilarating—I loved being there, thoroughly enjoyed working with the people who lived in the residence and those who came to Sunday service. More than four years had passed since I had moved to Ananda. At last, I had begun the ministry I dreamed of.

In retrospect, the months at the ashram with Rick, residents, and center members would seem an island in the midst of a long, arduous journey to self-awareness, a sojourn as idyllic as the glorious sunset I witnessed at Point Reyes.

Shiva's Trident

With sari-clad pilgrims,
Climb stone steps.
Ring bell—
Bow and wait—
A priest blesses the
Lei of golden flowers,
Murmurs prayer.
Stands—
Steps back—
Stretches up—
Impales my heart
On Shiva's Trident.

With fifty other pilgrims, residents and friends of Ananda, I travelled to Thailand and India. For three and a half weeks, we would travel to sites Paramahansa Yogananda had lived in and visited.

Our first stop was Bangkok, Thailand, where we visited the famous jade Buddha on the grounds of the marvelously ornate old palace, rode boats in the canals, and viewed a river park. On our second day, braving the jumbled traffic of downtown Bangkok, we shopped for souvenirs, visited a very large, gold Buddha in a very small temple, and attended a folk opera. Eager to get to India where our pilgrimage to the sites Yogananda had visited would begin, I paid little attention to the Thailand stopover; years later, I would be grateful that I had had the opportunity to visit this lovely land. Thailand is a beautiful and very special place.

The morning after our arrival in Delhi, India, we went by bus, through streets overflowing with people, automobiles, trucks, and cows, to the ashram of a famous swami. A temple official greeted us at the entrance and asked us to form into a double line. We set off immediately, winding our way through throngs of Indian devotees to an area apart from the main temple where masses of golden yellow flowers surrounded ornate images of the Divine Mother.

A dark-skinned, handsome man in his late forties, wearing the orange robes of a spiritual renunciate, stood to the right of the statues. He had uncombed, uncut, shining black hair; tiny, wiry curls thrust out from his head, forming a halo. I imagined he was the famous swami, though I was never to learn his name. As our group filed rapidly past, he blessed us, momentarily placing his hands on each of our heads.

To the left of the holy man, beside a golden pile of flowers, stood a monk. As we passed by, this man placed a garland of marigolds around our necks.

Thoroughly mystified, I followed the line of pilgrims to a small, bare room behind the main temple. Tiny overhead windows provided a dusky light; there were no furnishings. Indicating with a nod that we should be seated, the fifty of us in the tour group settled on the concrete floor. Our guide bowed and disappeared.

Jammed together on the floor in cross-legged positions, completely in the dark as to what we were waiting for, we chanted Sanskrit baijans, Indian devotional songs we sang at home at Ananda. Wherever we traveled, we carried with us a harmonium—a small, bellows-driven keyboard developed by Christian missionaries in India. Chanting before meditation was a part of daily life for most of us; in the Delhi temple, we fell into our customary way of song and prayer while we waited for the guide to return. After a half hour or so, the official returned with tea in little, disposable clay cups.

Before leaving America, to avoid illness, we had repeatedly been instructed not to accept food or drink in India. As guests in a holy place, we were in a quandary. Most of us swallowed our doubts and drank the tea; fortunately, none of the group became ill.

Then, suddenly, as quickly as we had arrived, we were whisked from the cramped hideaway to a raised platform six to eight feet above the floor of an enormous, open-air pavilion, and urged to continue chanting. Spread out below us in various positions of prayer and meditation, an enthusiastic crowd of several hundred responded with an outpouring of love and devotion for the Divine Mother.

Tightly packed together, sitting cross-legged on the dais, we had sung for perhaps a half an hour when several dark-skinned men wearing white dhotis and bearing armloads of flowers climbed onto the stage. Stepping over and around us, they draped more marigold leis around our shoulders.

We continued singing for another half hour before we left the temple. Passing through the throng of devotees, to avoid becoming separated, we held hands. Outside, we boarded the bus for the return to our hotel.

Moments later, on the streets of Delhi, my impressions of the temple, chanting, and deep devotion blended with a kaleidoscope of new sights and songs. Our visit to the shrine seemed a dream, a memorable experience in the shuffle of suffering humanity.

The next morning, we flew to Kashmir. At Dal Lake, handsome, young Muslim men rowed us from the shore to the houseboats we would occupy for three nights. Our morning meditations would be on a boat rooftop above the fog-draped lake. On the first day in Srinagar, after breakfast and a boat trip to shore, we visited an ancient Shiva temple atop Shankacharya Hill, east of the city. I felt I had come home.

Wanting to spend more time there than the schedule allowed, the following day a friend and I skipped a tour of a rug factory, hired a taxi, and returned to the mountaintop. I was dressed in a new, white sari I had purchased from a boat on the lake the previous evening. Around my neck, I wore a marigold mala that I had received at the Delhi temple. I intended to make it an offering to Shiva, the Unmanifest Creator god.

At the taxi drop-off, we purchased small packets of temple offerings before following the path a short way up the mountain and joining a long line of Indian pilgrims waiting to enter the temple compound. Overhead, a black Himalayan eagle circled gracefully, riding currents of air in a crisp blue sky. Two thousand feet below, shallow Dal Lake shimmered; in the distance, snow-clad Himalayan peaks ringed the high valley.

After an hour's wait, Nalini and I stepped over the stone lintel in the wall separating the inner temple from the surrounding hillside and began the slow climb up thirty feet of hollowed-out stone steps. Ashoka, an enlightened Indian leader who ruled around 230 BC, built the original structure. In the early seventeenth century, Mogul invaders constructed the present stone temple. Pilgrims had followed this path for more than twenty centuries. The antiquity of this site captured my heart.

At the temple door, as is customary, I rang the small, bronze bell suspended near the low entrance and stepped inside. Gleaming softly at the center of the dusky interior, a lingam—a chest-high, black, oval stone, signifying the male principal of God—rested in a shallow, four-foot-wide sandstone bowl, signifying the feminine principal of God. Above the sacred stone depicting the united power of Shiva and Shakti, Hindu masculine and feminine divinities, a flower-filled wire basket hung suspended from a ceiling rafter. From the basket, water dripped drop by slow drop onto the black lingam. A narrow passageway around the interior wall of the building permitted circumambulation of the holy image. Near the passageway, a shining brass cobra—symbol of the divine feminine energy, Shakti—rested.

At the side of the black stone lingam, a tiny Hindu priest crouched, chanting prayers. I waited several minutes until he opened his eyes and looked up. I handed him the small packets of salt and sugar, the traditional Indian offerings to the gods that I had purchased at the courtyard stand, then removed the golden flowers from around my neck and silently placed them in his small, dark hands. He nodded. For a moment, his eyes penetrated mine; then he closed his eyes and resumed chanting.

I did not know what I should do, so I waited for a cue from him. After praying for several minutes, he opened his eyes and stood up. Holding the marigold mala I had given him, he stepped to the back of the temple. Using a long pole and stretching as high as he could reach, the priest placed my flower offering on the three-pronged trident fork symbolizing Shiva's power as Creator, Sustainer, and Destroyer of the Universe.

White light filled my mind. My heart somersaulted. Time stopped.

His action totally surprised me. Stunned and overwhelmed with joy, I felt my self-offering had not only been accepted, it had been placed as close to heaven, to the highest God, as possible. The flowers were a representation of me; embraced by the divine, I was completely accepted.

> *One with Self,*
> *One with Silence.*
> *One with Shiva,*
> *The Unmanifest.*

Leaving Kashmir, we flew to Bubaneshwar. After staying overnight in a fine hotel, the next morning, I opened the blinds to see what the weather was like. White sheets and towels, which had been laid out to dry, dotted the banked lawn around the swank hotel.

From the hotel, we bussed to the little town of Puri on the Bay of Bengal. The spiritual essence of Yogananda's guru, Sri Yukteswar, permeated a Puri ashram on the Bay of Bengal. Here, amid perfumed tropical plantings,

Yogananda had studied with Yukteswar; years later, he had returned to this same location to officiate at Yukteswar's burial ceremonies.

As I meditated at the burial site, the Samadhi Mandir, I felt a detached, intensely focused intelligence, the same Shiva energy I had experienced at the Kashmiri temple. Pondering the connection between Shiva—the Boundless One—and Sri Yukteswar, a message telegraphed across my consciousness:

All your pain—
All your grief—
All your sorrow—
All the effort of a lifetime—
Never really happened.

Traveling with fifty other pilgrims, I felt I could not break down in tears. I managed to keep my composure as our group continued on the tour, first to the ancient shrine of Chaitanya—a fifteenth-century devotee of the Divine Mother—then south to the Lord Jagannatha temple surrounded by a high stone wall. Since Westerners were not permitted entry, we climbed a white, four-story wooden viewing stand across the street to look out over the temple and its grounds that occupied a several square-block area. Below, a steady stream of pedestrians, rickshaws, taxis, busses, and wandering cows passed along the broad boulevard.

Hours later, I took the window seat on the bus for our two-hour, sixty-mile return to Bubaneshwar and covered my face with a silk shawl. People would think I was meditating, but I planned to review the startling message I had heard at the Samadhi Mandir. Mentally, I repeated, *All your sorrow, all your pain never happened. All your grief, all your sadness never really happened.* How could that be?

Asha, one of the tour leaders asked, "Why are you crying?" I told her what I had heard. "What does it mean?" she asked. I could not explain. Today, I would answer her: Without personality—without the constructed ego, only pure consciousness—the Self—exists. In that openness—in that vast silence—no death, no loss, no pain occur. Only vibrant creativity.

For a fraction of second, I had gone beyond dual consciousness. In non-dual total awareness, what we feel in egoic consciousness disappears. Or, in the words of one of Paramahansa Yogananda's songs, *"No birth, no death, no caste have I. I am free, blessed spirit, I am free."*

Dakshineswar

In the *Autobiography of a Yogi*, Yogananda describes his visits to Dakshineswar, a temple dedicated to the Goddess Kali. There on the banks of the Ganges near Calcutta, Yogananda prevailed on the Blissful Mother to show herself, not giving up until he experienced her living presence.

When our group was there, we first visited and meditated in the quarters of Ramakrishna, the great turn-of-the-century master who lived at Dakshineswar when Yogananda prayed at the shrine of the Divine Mother. Afterward, in the temple square, we sat on a raised concrete platform in an open-air pavilion and chanted.

When the group began to meditate, I joined Indian pilgrims waiting for a glimpse of the Kali statue. I started toward the end of the line that circled the immense temple, but Yogananda's great-grandniece, who was traveling with us, intervened, putting me near the front of the long queue. Shoved forward by a crush of fervent devotees, I soon arrived at an opening in the temple wall. A priest raised the statue of the small, black goddess before me; I namasted; an attendant touched the point between my eyes with his middle finger, leaving a dot of red paint—a tilak.

Wherever I traveled in India, my gray hair and statuesque figure attracted attention, but never so much as at Dakshineswar. In general, Indians are smaller people, neither as tall nor as large in structure as North Americans, and during our entire Indian trip, I often marveled at how few Indian women had gray hair. In any case, a woman alone, especially an older woman, drew attention. Wearing a white cotton sari and the tilak, the red paint at the spiritual eye between my eyebrows, added to my unusual appearance. As I threaded my way through the crowd in the great square, people bowed and murmured, "Ma, Ma."

To escape the attention, which felt claustrophobic and embarrassing, I ducked into a souvenir market; even there, in a confined space, more people crowded around. Rescued by the shopkeeper, I found sanctuary in the first of twelve small temples on the Ganges riverbank that form the outer wall of the Dakshineswar temple compound. A little distance upstream, a busy, four-lane bridge spanned the river; in the temple, it was extraordinarily silent, so quiet I heard the river lapping on the shore.

The temple contained a Shiva lingam and a narrow walkway around the holy stone; immediately I decided to circumambulate the lingams in each of the twelve temples. I had visited six of the temples and was heading for the other six on the far side of the compound when a tour leader tapped me on the shoulder.

"Time to go," he said.

"All right," I answered. Standing in the middle of the square, I bowed six times, one for each of the remaining temples.

As I write, memory—as if Kali were dancing—flashes like a strobe light: images of women in jewel-colored saris; men in white dhotis and loose shirts; beautiful, quiet children at their sides. A gray stone lingam; yellow marigold malas; arching banyan tree roots; monkeys flying limb to limb. A bazaar selling holy trinkets; a goddess statue garmented in red and surrounded by masses of flowers. A wizened, bowing old man; snow-capped Himalayas; a tiny, gray-haired woman extending a creased palm; the Taj Mahal. Burning ghats; a gnarled tree beside the swift-flowing, mud-brown Ganges.

Now I ask … From that mélange of shifting impressions, could you have guessed your life had changed? That after India, nothing would be the same? That dancing Kali, the devastating black goddess, had entered your life?

FIFTY-FOUR (1986–1987)
THE GODDESS
Christmas

Early on the day before Christmas, with other center residents, I meditated in the basement temple. Dramatic change was occurring in the San Francisco ashram; I welcomed the quiet beginning to what I knew would be another very full day.

Challenge and sudden change were in the air; even the stars showed busyness. A challenging opposition lined up between Chiron (the wounded healer) in Gemini, and Saturn, Mercury, and Uranus (planet of sudden change) in Sagittarius. Squaring both points, Mars and Jupiter, the planet of the spiritual teacher and master, sat in Pisces.

After the meditation, I climbed two flights of stairs to the main floor and entered the kitchen where I toasted whole grain bread and filtered a cup of coffee. In the dining room, I pulled out a chair at a table next to the tall windows overlooking the Bay. From the library next door came the sound of a half-dozen voices rehearsing Swami Kriyananda's songs, preparing entertainment for fifty community members who would join us for dinner that evening.

I studied the wet view outside the bay windows. Three miles away, above billowing fog, the Golden Gate hung suspended. To the northeast, Angel Island drifted. I picked up the newspaper: rain through the day, adding water to the flooding I-5 corridor north of the city. I hoped my son Greg, a senior at Evergreen College, who would be driving through the area later in the day, would make it through without problems. Tomorrow, we would drive to Ananda with my eldest son Paul, who lived nearby, to spend Christmas with my daughter and son-in-law, David and Suzanne.

I finished breakfast, stacked my dishes in the dishwasher, and checked the bulletin board where I posted weekly housekeeping assignments. Everything seemed to be in order. To view the public rooms one last time, I entered the central hallway. A coat rack stood on the gleaming floor, ready to hold the overflow of outer garments. Matching settees flanked the blue-carpeted stairs to the upper floors. In the powder room, fresh towels had been hung.

In the broad entry to the front parlor, an altar with pictures of Christ and the gurus had been set up; in front of the altar sat the house harmonium. In the parlor interior, couches and chairs had been pushed against the walls to make room for folding chairs and meditation cushions. A crystal vase on the fireplace mantle held a bouquet of flowers, and Nancy would bring roses, the flower that Yogananda loved, for the altar.

Reentering the kitchen, I turned left through the narrow passageway behind the stove and slipped past Elizabeth as she reached for a jar of peppermint leaves. Another left turn took me up the stairs.

In my room, a bouquet of fully open, red roses—a gift from Swami Kriyananda—towered above pictures of the gurus and a bronze, dancing Shiva on the glass-covered coffee table that served as my altar. As I pulled the harmonium from under the table to practice chants for the meditation I would lead later in the day, I recalled the meeting with the center leader Rick Warner two weeks before.

"I'm going back to the farm," he had said.

I nodded. "What will you do?"

"I'm not sure. Maybe work in the garden. I need a rest."

"Who's going to replace you?"

"Swami hasn't decided."

After three years in the city ashram, Rick had earned a rest, but I would miss him. He was always supportive and genuinely appreciative of my help.

With Rick's eminent departure, we all wondered who the new ashram leader would be—I could not imagine being asked, nor did I want the responsibility. I did not think I had lived in the community long enough to attune to Yogananda's spiritual ray.

Swami named a couple, Naomi and Wayne, who had moved to the community the previous year. A long-time devotee who often visited Ananda, Naomi had owned and run a yoga center north of San Francisco before joining Ananda.

Downstairs, the phone rang—probably a guest calling about the meditation or dinner, I thought.

The knock at the door reminded me it was nearly time to begin the Christmas meditation. "Telephone," a man's voice said.

"I'll be right there." *Maybe it's Greg.* I hurried down the back steps and picked up the phone.

"Mrs. Garceau?" Ken, the student my son was traveling with, spoke softly. "Greg disappeared hours ago. I've waited as long as I can. Can I drop his things off at your house?"

I held my breath as Ken told me he had been sleeping while Greg drove. After he exited the freeway in heavy fog and pulled off the road, the shoulder gave way. Greg had gone to find a tow truck and had never returned. They had driven all night; Greg was tired and seemed confused.

Greg had been lonely in Washington after Stan and I moved to California, but whenever we urged him to live with us, he assured us he was fine. Like many young adults, he'd been slow to get his life on sure footing. Where could he be? Surely, he was all right.

I gave Ken hurried directions to the house and went into the living room to begin the four-hour, afternoon-long meditation. At each break, I checked for phone calls, but heard nothing more. Shortly after the meditation ended, Ken dropped off Greg's belongings. Our brief conversation prompted me to call the state patrol.

An hour later, as I was greeting dinner guests, an officer phoned. Earlier in the day, he reported, a disoriented man fitting Greg's description had approached a service station and asked for a tow, but since he had no money, the service was refused. The man was last seen hitchhiking south along the freeway. The state patrol would call if they received new information. Certain that the man he described was my son, I swallowed hard and went in to dinner.

After everyone left, I sat in the dark with Jill (a friend who had recently moved from the farm to the center) on the narrow stairs leading to my room. "There's no word," I said.

"Have you considered that he might be dead?"

"Yes," I whispered.

"Let's meditate," Jill said.

In my room, we sat on the edge of the bed facing the altar. After a few minutes, Jill left.

By morning, when nothing new had developed, I decided to go to Ananda where Greg was most likely to go, since he knew we were to celebrate Christmas there. Declining both Paul and Jill's offers to drive, because I needed the distraction to fend off my growing alarm, I guided the car onto the freeway and began the one-hundred-seventy-mile trip. Two and a half hours later, shortly after I turned off the freeway at Auburn, an owl took flight from a stand of oak trees a hundred yards left of the highway. Its four-foot black and white wings outstretched, the bird of prey swooped down to skim the hood of the car, inches from the windshield.

"I've never seen anything like that!" Jill exclaimed.

"Did you see how big it was?" Paul's voice filled the car.

"Shhh," I said. "The owl is speaking. I want to hear what it says."

As the car sped forward, I concentrated. Listening deeply into the depth of mental silence we cultivated in our daily meditations, I heard a voice repeating, "He's okay, he's okay." Seconds later, I exulted aloud, "Greg's okay, Greg's okay. He's alive! He's all right!"

Clinging to the message, I drove the last miles to Ananda. There, I joined Garth, my former student intern at Evergreen, at a table in the crowded Expanding Light. He looked dismayed when I told him about Greg being missing and the owl's message. "Let's talk later," he said.

At Suzanne and David's home, where we were to exchange gifts, Garth pulled me aside. Clasping my hands in his, he said, "Jo, don't you remember? The owl is a messenger of death. You must prepare yourself."

"I know, I know." I brushed tears from my eyes. "But my owl said Greg is safe."

"Let's get everyone together to pray," he said.

In the living room, Garth, Suzanne, David, Paul, and I held hands, forming a circle. We prayed briefly, then chanted Om. Less than a minute later, the phone rang.

Suzanne handed the receiver to me.

"Mrs. Garceau?" a male voice queried. "Will you accept a collect phone call from Greg?"

A Mistake

Greg had been found wandering and confused on the outskirts of Oakland. Picked up by the police and held for a hearing, he had then been remanded to a mental hospital for treatment. In the weeks that followed, I spent hours commuting back and forth across the Bay from San Francisco to Oakland, visiting my son, who would eventually be diagnosed with a chemical imbalance—very likely the result of his early childhood illness. Meanwhile, the direction of the ashram took a dramatic turn.

Soon after the new San Francisco ashram leaders arrived, Naomi told me that she and Wayne would handle the ministry. I was to keep house and manage the finances. The three of us would clean private homes in the city to cover personal expenses.

One afternoon, exhausted after a several-hour housekeeping job, followed by a two-hour trip across the Bay to visit Greg in the hospital, I returned home. When I entered my room, I found a large bouquet of five-petaled, pink and white stargazer lilies on the floor near the fireplace—a gift from a resident. The card read, "from Divine Mother." A heavenly fragrance filled the room.

Already in turmoil over my son's unexplained illness and the changes in the ministry, when Wayne told me he had received a call from a community leader saying that Greg could not stay at the center, the news overwhelmed me. I had spent nearly five years in the community, given body, mind, and soul to God, divorced, become assistant leader of a center, and now my son could not stay with me. I did not know where to turn.

One of my housekeeping clients invited both Greg and me to live with her until I could make other arrangements. When I told a community leader that I would have to leave the community to care for Greg, she agreed he could stay, provided there were no problems.

Some months earlier, Swami Kriyananda had announced that all five-year community members would automatically become assistant ministers. After another year, an individual was eligible to become a full minister. I would not be a six-year member for another eighteen months; yet, on a February visit, Swami Kriyananda said that while he was at the San Francisco ashram, he wanted to ordain the three of us. I was delighted. I did not question his decision.

In a private ceremony that evening, Naomi, Wayne, and I formally vowed to devote our lives and work to God and guru. Blessing each of us in turn, Kriyananda ordained us as Ananda ministers. Afterward, we joined Swami Kriyananda, his wife, Rosanna, and other Ananda ministers for a dinner celebration at a Thai restaurant a few blocks from the house.

The following week, during a gala reception at Crystal Clarity, Kriyananda's home at the farm, he beckoned me over to where he sat on a sofa. I bent over the coffee table in front of him and strained to hear his voice above the sounds of the noisy party. He said, "Jo, I made a mistake. I should not have ordained you—you must be an assistant minister for at least a year before becoming a full minister."

Not trusting my voice, I simply nodded.

He continued, "I'm making an exception for the others, since they're the center leaders. I'm sure you understand."

I nodded again. *God, don't let me make a fool of myself!* As soon as I could gracefully do so, I left the party.

ॐ

That winter, leader couples from the community, including Swami and Rosanna, frequently visited the center, offering support and guidance. The center leaders and I worked seven days a week. I was often up at five to lead a meditation; at times, the last devotee did not leave my room until after midnight.

When every bed was filled, forty-two people lived in the San Francisco ashram; to pay the six-thousand-dollars-a-month rent and buy groceries, we needed a full house. From week to week, sometimes from day to day, the roster of house residents changed. Long-time tenants moved out—some to the farm, others elsewhere. New people, some who flirted with spirituality and others who were serious devotees, joined us. Guests came and went.

In April, my son Greg began work in Marin County across the Bay. Medicines stabilized his mood fluctuations, and hard labor—laying railroad ties on a steep hillside—helped improve his mental and physical well-being. Life resumed a degree of normalcy.

Greg's astrological chart compared to the transits for that time suggested a particularly stressful period. I noted that the planets under stress in his chart were located at the exact point of my own ascendant. Clearly, we had a karmic connection; a difficult time for both of us, Greg was meant to be the source of spiritual growth for me, one that would continue years into the future. We are given tests in life; some of my greatest challenges and finest rewards have come through my youngest child.

Independence Day

On the eve of Independence Day 1987, Wayne, Naomi, and I were invited to a gathering at the farm, to be followed by a special San Francisco leaders' meeting. When I asked Wayne what the meeting was to be about, he said, "All I know is Naomi got a phone call asking us to be there." There was no intimation that anything was amiss.

This is heaven, I thought, as I drove from the city to Suzanne and David's home. I can attend the meetings, play with my two-and-a-half-year-old grandson, see friends, and rest for four whole days.

During my meditation the following morning, chaotic energy unlike anything I had experienced in more than fifteen years of spiritual practice, coursed up my spine. I felt a foreboding, as if a cyclone were about to strike. The feeling was so intense that I wondered, Is this the destructive energy of Kali, the fierce black goddess who wears a necklace of skulls and dances on Shiva's prone body?

Mystified by the disturbing meditation, I noted it in my journal before walking over to the center leaders' meeting at a nearby group home. As I passed newly built houses on both sides of the road, I puzzled over the powerful, dark, and intense energy—the gale-force winds of change that had swept through my psyche. They were totally unexplainable. I had no reference point.

Two hours later, I learned the purpose of the meeting was to discuss the San Francisco center leadership and living cooperatively. I was reprimanded for having a bad attitude and told that unless I changed, I would never again do anything for Ananda.

I was devastated. As I heard the words, a black velvet curtain filled my mind. My consciousness spiraled down into utter darkness and I sobbed like a child. The others present gathered around me and prayed, but I could not be consoled. I died.

Kali, in her inimitable fashion, had cut away my dependence on external authority.

FIFTY-FOUR TO FIFTY-SEVEN (1987–1990) DANCING WITH KALI

"A collapse of the conscious attitude is no small matter. It always feels like the end of the world, as though everything had tumbled back into original chaos. One feels delivered up, disoriented, like a rudderless ship that is abandoned to the moods of the elements. So at least it seems. In reality, however, one has fallen back upon the collective unconscious, which now takes over the leadership."

—Carl Jung, from Two Essays on Analytical Psychology (Collected Works, Vol. 7)

Everything I had built my life on fell into disarray. My self-confidence was gone. I had no foundation. Trying to determine what had gone wrong, I spoke with several women in leadership roles in the community—one who had been in a managerial position for many years, and two other ministers. Each told me I should remain at the San Francisco center and meditate to understand the important spiritual lesson I had been given.

On July 2, 1987, the day I was reprimanded for having a bad attitude, transiting outer planets Uranus, Saturn, and Chiron completed a grand square with the Virgo moon. Early that morning, the moon had passed both my south node and Jupiter, often referred to as the guru or master's signature. Here, again, destiny was at work resolving old karma.

Chiron is a healing planet ruling the collective unconscious, the underworld; Uranus reflects sudden divine intervention; Saturn structures and puts matters into place in the mundane world. It is noteworthy that Chiron, the wounded healer, was conjunct Venus, signature of the feminine, that day. Taken in its entirety, the chart reflects spiritual energies coming to a climax, all signaling dramatic change in one's sense of the feminine self, or perhaps the feminine being healed through great conflict, or the feminine herself bringing healing. This would confirm my belief that Kali, the great goddess of discrimination and destruction, was active.

The grand square thus formed between transiting and natal signatures challenged my old way of behaving, which I brought with me from previous lifetimes. Because Jupiter, the spiritual teacher, was so prominent in this conjunction, one must conclude that a great spiritual lesson was intended.

By November, four months after the reprimand, I had decided that nothing held lasting reality. True, I breathed in and out—but my breath could stop any time. True, too, the sun rose every day and would likely rise for millennia. On the other hand, at any moment, a meteor strike or some other catastrophe could destroy the earth. Nothing had reality; nothing was permanent; and nothing was mine.

I began weekly trips to Point Reyes Seashore, thirty miles north of San Francisco, where I hiked the trails and memorized the shoreline. Chimney Rock, an isolated landmass jutting out on the southern end of the main peninsula, became my refuge. Surrounded by the pounding waves of the Pacific Ocean on the west, protected by Drake's Bay on the east, the promontory high above the sea offered a perfect sanctuary for my bruised heart.

I began counseling that fall with a Buddhist monk, a transpersonal psychologist. The following spring, I retreated to family property in central Oregon. There, every day for two months, I walked miles, meditated for hours, and journalled. What was I to do? Follow Paramahansa Yogananda? Abandon ten years of my life and leave the community?

While I vacillated, I received an invitation to join Ananda's board of directors. Perhaps, I thought, as a member of the board, I can observe community decision-making; with more information, my direction may become clear.

I returned to the farm. For the next eighteen months, I freelanced as an independent bookkeeper, avoided community involvement, devoted myself to meditation, and made monthly trips to San Francisco to see Greg and my therapist.

My San Francisco counselor said I reminded him of the Fool card in the Tarot deck—knapsack on my back, puppy nipping at my heels, headed into life without a clue. At his suggestion, I began asking, "Who am I? What is my purpose? What prevents me from achieving my goal?" As days, then months passed, the questions became a mantra I asked over and over. Hour by hour, the answer changed.

Who am I? Not this. Not that. What is my purpose? Now this, now that. When my identity changed, my purpose shifted; when my purpose changed, my identity shifted. Nothing lasted. Nothing was permanent.

A few years earlier, the class I attended on the *I Ching* had changed my thinking; I had consulted the Book of Change daily for several years and gradually concluded that life was only change. Everything changes; nothing is constant except for change. I had known this before the reprimand, yet I had not fully embraced the idea. I—consciousness—identity—changed from moment to moment.

And the obstacles? Sometimes outside myself, sometimes coming from within, the barriers changed as my identity and purpose changed.

Life—who I was—was ephemeral, a flowing river.

After having met with him for well over a year, my therapist reminded me of an old story about a boatman carrying passengers from one side of a river to the other. He asked, "When you reach the other shore, why do you need the boat?"

He implied that I had no need for spiritual teachers, that I had grasped the Truth. I certainly did not feel that way. Confused and unattached, I felt as if I were a ship without a rudder. I did not live in bliss; nor did I see lights and angels or bless others by my presence. I was the lost pariah. Perhaps I did not need to live in the community, but I needed support.

I began to prefer being alone and silent. The culture and my family upbringing had demanded that I be other-oriented, an extrovert who cared for others before myself. Now, I discovered that I loved silence—the space Paramahansa Yogananda referred to when he counseled, *Silence is the altar of God.* As I rebuilt my shattered identity, my truer introverted nature emerged. I became a hermit.

One evening after my return to Ananda, during the winter of early 1989, as usual I meditated before falling asleep. Just after midnight, a buzzing sensation—a steady flow of energy—coursed throughout my body and woke me. For several hours, I rested in a state of aware sleep, while the vibration—which I thought to be healing—continued.

The following morning, my daughter Suzanne, who was employed in another business a half mile from where I worked, phoned. She needed to talk. Wondering what was so urgent, I agreed to meet her for lunch. Sitting in winter sunshine at a picnic table outside the building where she did accounting, she told me, "Dad was injured last night. He's in critical condition in a Los Angeles hospital; for several hours early this morning, doctors operated on him. He may not live."

I had never regretted the end of our marriage, but I did not want my former husband to die with anything unresolved between us. That evening, I telephoned him in the hospital. As we spoke, his voice grew stronger; from gloom, he turned to laughter. When I hung up, he seemed remarkably better. In fact, he fully recovered. Later, I learned that the healing I had experienced during the previous night had occurred during the entire four-hour period of his operation. It seemed that at some level, even after our divorce, the connection between us remained.

As I continued therapy, I began to feel that I wanted more than what Ananda offered—though more of what, I could not say. Meeting with my therapist helped to resolve my despair, but I was no longer creative. During a visit in late spring the following year, I was shocked when he told me, "You've been clinically depressed since I met you eighteen months ago."

Later in the same session, he said, "Your father encouraged you."

"Yes," I agreed. "I loved my father."

"So your need for love, your dependency, took the form of independence."

"I don't understand."

"Have you considered the possibility that you developed your independent nature to please your father? That you are not really independent, but always seek approval?"

For hours after the session, I wandered the streets of San Francisco, weeping, agonizing over my desire for validation and my needy caretaker response. Yes, I took care of people. Yes, I had led. Yes, I had been the family breadwinner, raised four children, carried enormous responsibility in state government, and then moved to Ananda—but these accomplishments had largely occurred under the guise of independence. I needed to be needed. Longing for love determined my behavior.

Dependent on others for love, I had given up the direction of my life. No wonder I was chronically depressed!

Two years after the reprimand, I still pondered new directions. What part of me made decisions? How could I decide? Slowly, I stumbled toward clarity.

Follow Your Dream

The decision to go on a Vision Quest followed a visit with my therapist. I had stayed overnight with Greg, who had moved to the Palo Alto ashram to be near his work with a computer company, and after lunch the following day, had driven to Point Reyes and hiked to Chimney Rock, a small point of land on the main peninsula. Completely isolated, for hours I had lain in the tall grass, surrounded by bountiful spring bloom. Waves crashed on the shore below; overhead, cormorants and seagulls circled in a faultless blue sky. Eventually, I had meditated, and after sunset, I had made the three-hour drive back to the farm.

Vision Quest

In indigenous cultures around the world, young adults are often sent out into the wilderness under austere conditions to find their personal direction. In Western American cultures, these sometimes take the form of several days alone without food or water. Under the stress, an individual may learn his/her life destiny.

A few days later, I mentioned to one of Suzanne's housemates how at home I felt in nature. She suggested that I might want to go on a Vision Quest, like those undertaken by American Indians. The following day, an advertisement in an alternative paper caught my attention; it seemed like a sign from heaven. I phoned and spoke with the doctoral candidate at the Institute of Transpersonal Psychology in Palo Alto who would lead the venture. He sent materials, and I immediately signed up for the trip to Joshua Tree National Monument in the Southern California desert.

The week before the Vision Quest, I was preparing for the trip. As I pulled my car to a stop, a squirrel scampered across the vacant parking lot and up the bank in front of the car. I got out, stretched, and looked around the closed fishing resort at the base of Sierra Butte in California's Sierra Nevada Mountains. Wind sighed in the Ponderosa pines; overhead, clouds scattered across an opal sky. Occasional birdsong broke the silence.

I had begun a fast two days before; now I shivered in the chill June air. I would be cautious. I needed to watch closely for weather changes.

Settling my daypack on my shoulders, I snapped the waist buckle shut and began the hike up the rutted, rock-strewn track that cut between knee-high bushes and massive granite blocks. Here and there, coral-red Indian paintbrush and clumps of pink-purple flowers grew along the banks of the primitive road. As I climbed higher, the surface of the lake on my left appeared to drop slowly below me.

Half a mile up the trail, the ground leveled out. Immediately east, in a grassy meadow that dropped precipitously into a canyon, the whitened trunk of an ancient cedar emerged from a shale ledge, twisted a hundred feet up to scraggly branches, and ended in a bare, broken top.

I crossed the meadow and stood on tiptoe on a boulder resting near the edge of the canyon. Balancing cautiously, I stretched to reach a sprig of fragrant cedar. I would take it on the Vision Quest I had signed up for.

Back on firm ground, I considered the darkening skies above snow-covered Sierra Butte. At its base lay Upper Sardine Lake, reflecting the sheered-off side of the towering mountain and its several-thousand-foot rocky fall. Near me, at the east end of the lake, pristine water cascaded from an earthen dam into the meadow, meandered past the old cedar, then tumbled through a slot in a granite wall. From there, the stream gurgled and danced five hundred feet down a slope to enter the lower lake. Miles south across the lower lake, mountain ranges shaded from green to blue to purple as they grew more distant, then disappeared into the curve of the earth.

Mountains had always signaled new peaks for me to scale, obstructions to surmount. Since I had encountered my own personal Everest two years before, I had vacillated about leaving Ananda. Again and again, wrestling with my twin desires to be spiritual and to remain true to my Self, I went over the trip to India, Greg's illness and recovery, the change of leadership at the San Francisco center, and the shocking leadership meeting. *What could I have done differently? Should I leave?*

Tucking the sprig of cedar in my daypack, I left the meadow. Three hundred yards up the trail, I paused where Garth and I had camped eight years before. I was so sure my spiritual calling was to Ananda. *Now, I wonder if the direction I so keenly felt was simply a call to a new beginning.*

As the morning hours lengthened into afternoon, I meandered along the shore of the upper lake. Following an unusual birdcall, I discovered a canyon wren perched on the branch of a leafing tree; scattered wildflowers, the shape of a stone, and shifting light on the lake all spoke to me. *My dream of helping people has shattered, but Nature herself calls me to ministry.*

Eventually, I hiked to the top of the ridge to view miles and miles of blue lakes and mountain ranges overshadowing pine-forested valleys. On my right, snow-crested Sierra Butte rose. On my left, far below at the distant trailhead, my car, a barely discernable white speck, waited. The wind gusted, and the clouds thickened. Beads of ice hit the ground and bounced; the terrain around me turned white. Time to turn back.

From my pack, I took a blue, plastic rain slicker and slipped it over my sweater. Pulling a wool fisherman's cap over my ears, I reversed direction. On the way down, I picked bunches of pink manzanita teardrops and, for sheer pleasure, embraced a massive rock. At a switchback, I wrapped my arms around a magnificent five-hundred-year-old pine—a giant so big around, my hands did not meet one another.

At the car, I pulled off my hiking boots and slipped on soft leather shoes. Sipping water from my old army canteen, I scanned the area one last time— blue lake, snow-covered butte, purple mountains, pink and olive manzanita bushes, granite boulders, pine green forest—a superb place for introspection, a fine spot to prepare for a Vision Quest. I was ready. Stowing my pack on the passenger side of the vehicle, I slid into the driver's seat.

The motion of the car and the turn of the wheel on steep mountain curves focused my attention. I drove for several minutes. Just after I rounded a series of hairpin turns, my inner voice spoke: *Don't go to the mountain top. Live simply in the valley. Follow your dream.*

Desert Journey

On a Sunday afternoon in mid-June, I parked my car at a trailhead in Joshua Tree National Monument. It had been less than a month since I had responded to the advertisement offering a three-day Vision Quest in the Southern California desert.

After backpacking a mile into an oasis—two old palms swaying in a gentle breeze and a small grassy area, Brian and his partner Nancy, Diane, and I set up base camp. Less than an hour later, each carrying a gallon plastic milk jug filled with water, we set out under a blazing hot sun to choose our sites in the desert.

My Vision Quest partner, Diane, a slender woman in her mid-forties, and I circled east and south. Avoiding cacti barbs, we gingerly picked our way up and down ridges and over boulders, following vague animal trails, before separating to select our individual sites.

While hiking in the northern Sierra Nevada's on the previous Saturday, my inner voice had told me to seek valleys, so I headed toward a natural bowl about an eighth of a mile in diameter with a stone outcropping on its northern perimeter that would afford some protection. From the low stone overhang, the land sloped gently south. Thirty miles west, across a desert valley, the San Jacinto Mountains peaked in an indigo sky. To the east, a five-hundred-foot mountain lifted skyward. It seemed the perfect spot.

Gathering large stones, I carried them to a broad, open space and marked the four directions of the prayer circle where I planned to spend the last night of the Vision Quest praying for guidance. Just as I set the last rock, a raven cawed. I looked up to see the bird fly over, black feathers gleaming in the late afternoon light. Its shadow flashed across the circle and continued south. *A good omen*, I thought. *Sacred medicine—the courage to enter the void.*

Leaving my water jug at my site next to the rock outcropping, as Brian had instructed, I rejoined Diane for the return to base camp.

After supper, the four of us settled around a campfire. "In the morning," Brian told us, "take two gallons of water with you to your site. That, plus the one you left this afternoon, should be enough. If you need more, I've cached water on the ridge. Look for it on your way out in the morning."

"What kinds of animals are out there?" Diane asked.

After adding wood to the blaze, Brian answered, "Snakes, spiders, scorpions, rabbits, maybe even a wild cat." He paused, "I've been on a half-dozen Vision Quests. Animals have never been a problem. They'll respect your territory."

Not only will I mark my territory, I thought, *I'll watch for signs; their appearance could indicate my future direction.*

"I'm afraid my body can't handle a fast in desert temperatures," I admitted.

"We all need to discover and accept our limitations," Brian said.

Guess I'll do all right, I thought as I crawled into my backpacking tent. *Four years ago, I ran eighteen miles in a jogathon; seven years ago, Suzanne, David, and I climbed Mount Adams. Even if I don't have the stamina of a twenty-five-year-old, I should be all right.*

At dawn, the haunting sound of a reedy flute woke me. I stuffed a few things into my pack, pulled on long cotton pants, socks, and hiking boots, and exited my tent on all fours. Dew dampened my knees and glistened on the leaves of nearby bushes; a hundred feet away, tattered palm fronds rustled in a light breeze.

At the edge of the grass, Brian bent, setting rocks. Pack on my back and a gallon of water in each hand, as the sun tipped over the horizon, I stepped into the circle he had just created. Rotating a smoldering bundle of cedar and sweet grass slowly up, down, and around my body, Brian prayed, "May you see your path clearly." Then he whispered, "For three days, enter the circle of invisibility."

Brian completed the ritual for Diane and we left the base camp in silence, noting the water cache amid rocks and cacti fifty yards up the trail. Topping the hill, we dipped into a gully, then made our way up a steep incline to a cluster of giant boulders midway between our sites.

There, we built a small rock pile to serve as our life support system. I would change the mound each evening; Diane would change it every morning. If one of us failed to remove or add stones to the pile, the other would search for her and bring help. We silently hugged; Diane began the ascent up a steep trail to the top of a five-hundred-foot hill, and I headed west.

From the stone circle I had set out the previous evening, I went south to a twelve-foot granite stone, the tallest object in the natural bowl I had chosen. As I set up camp below the ancient monolith, securing a gray nylon tarp to rocks at the sides of the sandy wash and a tall mesquite bush on the west, a sand-colored lizard darted from under its pencil-thin branches and slithered into the shadow of surrounding rocks. I wondered what messages the lizard, symbol of dreaming the future, would bring.

My camp established, I settled in under the tarp. Except for the buzzing of an occasional bee in the delicate yellow mesquite flowers, the desert lay quiet. Slow hours passed, and tiny movements became events: a butterfly's gold and black wings fluttered against the underside of the gray nylon tarp; a hummingbird flew in from the west side of the shelter and out its east side. The desert spoke to me: bees, symbol of the divine feminine; butterfly, symbol of transformation; and hummingbird, carrier of prayers to heaven.

At sunset, I hiked to the rock pile, marked it, collected the water left at the stone circle, and returned shaking and panting to camp. As night fell, I sat outside the shelter, enjoying the breeze. *How silly this seems! Why am I here—hot, hungry, and weak? I could get up, walk into base camp, say good-bye, and leave.* But I would not …

I built a tiny fire and boiled water. Sipping tea, I watched the waxing moon rise in the star-washed sky. In my journal I wrote, "A strange way to pray; no words, only silence."

I dreamed that I met a couple in a second-hand store, buying another person's vision. I told the couple, "For most of my life, I embraced other people's spirituality. Now, my guidance comes direct from God."

At first light, I sat with my back against the granite slab at the head of the wash. *If my guidance comes from God, I thought, why do others decide how I live?*

When the sun rose above the rock, I retreated to the shelter of the tarp. The temperature climbed. Sipping tea from a cup left in the sun, I burned my tongue. Occasional breezes stirred, but never enough for relief. Eventually, in the late afternoon, wispy clouds obscured the sun, and the desert began to cool.

Feeling stronger, I went first to the rock pile and then to the prayer circle. Yearning for greenness—if the desert was a metaphor for interior dryness, green represented new growth—I hiked south in a gully until I found a bottle-green salt cedar rooted deep in the parched soil. As I approached, a golden butterfly fluttered up.

As I resumed my walk, a timid jackrabbit burst from its hiding place and scampered ahead. Near a rock fall, the droppings of a small wild cat lay beside the track—a good omen! The secretive animal would avoid being seen; its presence portended the revelation of a hidden aspect of myself. I reversed direction and returned to camp.

In my sleep that night, I felt loved—supported and surrounded by a spirit, embraced by the desert silence. Toward morning, I dreamed. *A woman demanded, "Betty Jo, pick that up!" I'm not Betty Jo! I thought. My mind spun. Then a motherly, dark-skinned woman held out an enormous armful of green leaves and herbs. "Betty Jo," she said, "these are yours."*

That morning, I again sat in the granite slab's cool shade. A gray lizard darted from the shadows; a yellow hummingbird hovered nearby. *Like these modest creatures,* I thought, *the dream is telling me to be practical and down to earth ...*

The dream woman reminded me of my Indian heritage and my great-great-grandparents who had lived at Fort Vancouver in the mid-nineteenth century. Then and there, wanting to claim my Indian heritage, I decided to change my name. Since I wanted to keep my children's surname, I would combine my maiden and married names: Jo Mills Garceau.

The third day was even hotter than the previous days. Despite drinking a large amount of water and repeated sponge baths, my heart raced. For hours, I lay in the shade of the tarp with a wet cloth over my eyes, mind numb, willing myself to endure. Toward mid-afternoon, without forewarning or thought, as though powered by an unseen force, suddenly my right fist slammed into my cupped left hand, and my voice shouted, *"Give me courage, strength, and wisdom! I have to do what I came to do! I have to be who I am!"*

An hour before nightfall, I prepared to move to the stone circle. As I struggled to lift the pack onto my shoulders, salty sweat dripped into my eyes. Tears welled up. I wiped my brow and tried again. Finally, I got the pack on my back and began the gentle climb, but in less than thirty feet, I gagged and gasped; my heart pounded. I wondered if I would die.

What should I do? Surrounded by prickly pears, mesquite, and sand, I rested on a hot, flat rock and considered the options. *Time is running out ... I need to be in the circle before dark ... My son-in-law, David, taught me to take two breaths for every step when we climbed Mount Adams ... I'll try that.*

At the top of the long incline, ignoring all wilderness rules, I abandoned my pack and water—I just could not carry them further—and went to check the rock pile. *I don't have the strength to climb the mountain to search for her ... Thank God! She moved a rock; she's okay!*

Retracing my steps, I picked up my gear and carried it the last one hundred fifty feet to the stone circle. Too exhausted to conduct the ceremonies I had planned, I lay down and closed my eyes.

The light of the full moon woke me.

Pale light shadowed mesquite and cacti and softened the jagged surfaces of the granite outcropping behind me. The starry sky spread east over Diane's five-hundred-foot peak, south to Mexico, west to the San Jacinto's, and north into the Great Basin. A shooting star in the west streaked earthward; its twin flashed across the eastern sky.

I slept, I woke, I slept again.

I dreamed: *On the fifth floor of a movie studio, an actor plays a part. "Nellie, forgive me," he pleads.*

For all my life, I thought, *a male imposter has spoken for me, pretending to be my real self. Now, he asks forgiveness.*

In the false light of dawn, I climbed a hundred feet to the top of the ridge behind the stone circle. Kneeling, I scooped out a shallow hole, placed in it a sprig of incense cedar and the healing crystal—the Herkimer diamond I had carried for years, and covered them with sand. Committing myself to follow the guidance I had received in dreams, I sent blessings to the world. I prayed the crystal would be a receiving station, transmitting healing to the world for as long as it remained there.

A half-mile away, a tiny figure descended the trail from the crest of Diane's mountain. I returned to the prayer circle, lifted my pack onto my back, and began a new journey.

Six months later, I left Ananda.

The astrological signatures for the preparation and time in the desert are dramatic, when compared to my natal chart. On one side of my chart, in the fifth house of creativity, Uranus (planet of the celestial world and the voice of God or sudden inspiration) combines its energies with the Moon, Neptune (another planet of the celestial realm, which signals expansion of consciousness), the house of Pisces and the home of the Bodhisattva, and Saturn. Considering all the celestial influence, one can readily see that Saturn was making a great effort to ground that inspiration in an everyday way. In my case, these planetary energies united in the house of creativity, the house where I believe, ultimately, we are creatively forming our selves.

Across the chart, in the eleventh house of groups and organizations—one might say the Ananda spiritual community—Chiron (the wounded healer) and Venus (planet of the feminine) were situated. Energy I had previously devoted to large political organizations and then to a spiritual community was being rerouted to focus on the self and creativity. The emphasis was on individual growth, not service to the group. During this entire cycle, five planets moved through Gemini at the mid-heaven, emphasizing communication as well as my contribution to society. Uranus and Saturn, especially, spoke. "I have to be who I am; I have to do what I came to do!"

Seven months later, on January 13, 1990, the day I drove north from Ananda to Portland where I would make my new home, the Sun and Mercury had joined Uranus, Neptune, and Saturn in the fifth house of creativity. This unusual stellium of outer planets, the Sun, and Mercury urged me to spiritual expression in a singular way.

The Divine Feminine

○ ○

"We are the mothers of the new consciousness. We are virgins empowered in the ever-present, ever-evolving images of Now. We are crones trusting the unknowable. Mother, virgin, crone, nature open to the fire of the imagination ... affirming our own I AM."

—*Marion Woodman, from Leaving My Father's House*

FIFTY-SEVEN TO SIXTY-THREE (1990 - SUMMER 1996)

A PERSONAL PATH
If You Will Stand Up, I Will See You

If moving from Olympia had been difficult, leaving the spiritual community was more so. The ambitious journey begun in joy had culminated in the dark night of the soul. Now, three years shy of sixty, I left Ananda and the path of transcendence to follow my personal path. I thought it would be a path of ordinariness, a search for like-minded souls. Ultimately, I hoped to find a new understanding of my connection to the ineffable. Always conscious of the mandate I had heard at eight, I expected to find ways to be of service to others.

On a sunny May morning that first spring in Portland, as I crossed the Markham Bridge high above the Willamette River, I became aware of a subtle inner presence. *That's my self*—I thought with a start—*small, hidden, and cautious. Yet, how wonderful! She has the rest of my life to grow!*

113

The more this inner child—the true feminine—revealed herself, the happier I became.

A full two years after I left Ananda, I dreamed that I still lived there. *In the center of the usual community bustle, I greeted a busload of Japanese pilgrims and accompanied their wizened holy man into a hall for a performance. From behind the stage curtains, a community leader orchestrated the celebration. Busy with the preparations, Anandans were unaware of the depth of the pilgrims' awareness.*

When the arrangements were complete, the leader appeared. As if he were God the Father, Almighty, he blessed me—my conversation with the Japanese elder pleased him. But I was having none of it. I was not there to please him; I was befriending a man with whom I felt spiritual kinship.

I woke in a pillow-pounding rage. How dare this arrogant male approve me? Angry with the patriarchal father-God the man represented, I yelled, "Get out! I am tired of your demands. I don't believe in you! Somebody made you up—I won't obey you any longer!"

A few days later, Sharon, the friend who had accompanied me on my first visit to Ananda more than ten years before, visited. As we strolled in a nearby park, I told her of my dream. In another synchronous event, when we returned to my home, a small, white Buddha figure I had purchased in Thailand lay on the floor amid glittering purple shards of the curved piece of amethyst I had used as its backdrop. The amethyst had burst into hundreds of pieces and scattered across the carpet.

"My image of God has shattered," I exclaimed. "Men will never again define what I do."

Years before, my thesis mentor, Dr. John McGee, had asked why I believed in a male God and yet espoused feminine issues. Now ten years after I met with him and after leaving Catholicism and Ananda, I finally unmasked the father-God of my psyche. At last, the Omniscient Male Being who permeated Mother's and my life with guilt, judgment, and damnation— the great and powerful Wizard of Oz—was gone. Before, if I dared to think and act for myself, he had thundered hell and brimstone. Now, he was gone. Dear old Auntie Em—a warm, loving Divine Mother—had replaced him.

And beyond that? The Mystery, deeper, more sublime—neither god nor goddess—simply Presence. Compassion, Wisdom, and Silence.

On a crisp winter morning in 1994, I walked briskly to work across the Hawthorne Bridge. Light from a late-rising sun glowed on the river's western bank in front of me. One after the other, huge flocks of starlings flew from the steel bridge scaffolding above, creating an undulating black ribbon in the sky. Beneath the bridge, currents ruffled the surface of the river. Downstream, behind a barge, waves rippled across the quiet stream. Car after car passed, tires humming on the grated steel deck. Bells rang as bicycles flitted by, and riders called, "Passing on your left."

Halfway across, the river expanded to encompass the greater proportion of all that I saw—and, suddenly ... *I was the traffic on the bridges, the concrete abutment beside the stream, and wispy long clouds in the expanse of blue sky. I was the Portland Spirit docked below cascading Tom McCall fountain and the red and white sternwheeler securely roped to steel anchors. I was posh apartments, boats in the marina, the Ross Island Bridge, and the river passing Oaks Bottom.*

A few days later, I described this experience to a therapist with whom I had been meeting. She exclaimed, "You've transcended!"

But—after ten years at Ananda, I associated transcendence with the shattering of self. I wanted validation for who I was, not congratulations for escaping ordinary life. Escaping into spirit had been too painful. Transcendence felt like seduction—a flight from my real self.

Cerridwen and Cernunnos

A month or two later, a dream woke me: *From a busy city street, I enter a small, round, stone temple. Feeling my way in total darkness down three flights of steps, I arrive at a heavy, wood door. Opening it, I step into a sunlit garden. In the center of this Eden, on an earthen mound, a plump woman wearing a yellow dress embossed with golden butterflies sits. From her head, a green fern grows.*

Her partner—a slender, tall man—wears a topknot of gray hair from which a long tendril of ivy dangles. Bowing deeply from the waist, he welcomes me. He explains that he and the woman are magicians in town for a special performance, and invites me to their show the next evening.

"How will you know me?" I ask.

"If you will stand up, we will see you."

Instantly, I am seated in the upper rows of a large coliseum among thousands of cheering people. I stand up. Far below, from the most distant arena of a three-ring circus, the couple waves.

I woke shouting, "It's Cerridwen!"

But who was Cerridwen, and who was the man accompanying her, this odd couple with plants growing from their heads? Did I read her name somewhere? I could not recall ever having heard of her. At two in the morning, I began searching through the books in my library for some evidence that she had existed.

In an hour, I had learned that Cerridwen, the Welsh Mother Goddess always shown with a creative cauldron, appeared in three aspects: maiden, mother, and crone. According to legend, after Cerridwen brewed a pot of magic, then boiled it down to a potent three drops, the boy who stirred the kettle stole the precious elixir. When Cerridwen discovered the theft, the goddess chased the lad through heaven and earth. Taking on numerous guises and god-like aspects, he escaped. Eventually, he became Taliesin, bard and magician, and in still later tales, Cernunnos, Cerridwen's consort.

My research revealed that Cernunnos, a chthonic god of fertility, appears on the Gundestrup Cauldron, a second-century-BC silver sacrificial bowl found in a European peat bog in 1891. Considered the finest ancient Celtic archeological item ever recovered, the bowl depicts Cernunnos surrounded by animals and vegetation, meditating in yogic posture. A horned god, he holds symbols of male power and female wisdom.

I associated Cernunnos with Shiva, the Supreme Indian God, a personification of the Unmanifest Self, who wears a topknot and perpetually meditates. Drawing from the collective consciousness preceding the cultures of both Northern Europe and the Indian sub-continent, my archetypal dream signaled the eventual inner marriage of masculine and feminine. The dream encouraged my feminine self to grow more confident, to stand up and be seen. Significantly, I had always loved Shiva, and in my dream, he was in service to the feminine goddess.

Our Lady of Guadalupe

Crossing the brick courtyard that separated the monks' enclosure from guest facilities at Our Lady of Guadalupe Trappist Monastery near Lafayette, Oregon, I entered the church foyer and passed through swinging doors into the long, narrow sanctuary. Slipping into a crowded pew, I knelt and removed a hymnal from the back of the bench in front of me.

Behind a railing that divided the public from the monks and priests, beneath the high arched ceiling, the altar stood. Seated on stools around the altar, a dozen priests, ranging from forty to eighty years of age, waited to concelebrate Mass. From a doorway on the left behind them, monks in white robes hurried into the church from the monastery. In an alcove on the right, a monk played the opening notes of a hymn; behind him, a half-dozen monks stood, holding songbooks in their hands. Seconds later, the presiding priest entered. On the organ's full-throated cue, the congregation rose to sing the opening hymn.

After Mass, while the monks and priests mingled with visitors, I walked around the grounds to see what was new since my last visit. Before I moved to California, the abbey did not accommodate women guests; during the years I was away from the Northwest, four of the sixteen rooms were dedicated to women's use. After I returned to Portland, I began visiting the abbey one Saturday a month; this would be my first weeklong stay. Because the monastery was so popular, I had reserved my room in February, eight months earlier.

Although the abbot and many of the monks had combined traditional Christian prayer with Eastern meditation since the late 1970s, the community only recently had built a zendo—a Japanese Buddhist prayer space, connected by a covered walkway to the main church. The simple structure contained a coatroom, a hall where monks and guests gathered monthly for daylong Zen sittings, and a meditation area for daily sittings. There, firm, black cushions rested in precise rows on mats facing floor-to-ceiling windows overlooking the lawn and forest.

On the crest of a slope near the eastern wall of the monastery, twelve tombstones marked the burial places of monks who had died since 1957, the year the community moved from Arizona to Oregon. The graves seemed to say that a monk's life—like everyone's—begins and ends in the eternal now. In the parade of days, light and shadow blend. Life becomes an anthem to the creator, to the glory of transcendence, to the transience of daily rising and lying down again.

After a simple meal with three women and two men—all guests for the week, a monk assigned me a room on the second floor of the women's lodge. Entering the plainly furnished room, I raised the venetian blinds. I wanted to be as close as possible to nature. I missed the countryside.

At five, I joined three other guests for meditation with Brother Mark in the zendo. A tall man in his late fifties, the traditional Trappist garb—white calf-length robe and black cloth apron, encircled by a heavy, leather belt—draped his spare frame. Below the hem of his wool garment, hairy legs and feet extended; because Birkenstock sandals are easy to slip into and out of, even on the coldest days, Brother Mark wore an old pair with scuffed over heels.

After the usual supper of leftovers from the midday meal, I returned to the church for vespers. Behind the main altar, beyond the monks' entry from the monastery, benches faced one another across a broad aisle; there, five times a day the monks chanted and prayed. On the rear wall of the sanctuary, above the original, pre-Vatican II church altar, a large image of Our Lady of Guadalupe hung. Venerated throughout the Americas, the picture depicts the Divine Mother as she appeared on the robe of Juan Diego, the Mexican peasant who miraculously met her on a wintry, sixteenth-century morning.

At vespers, accentuating the presence of the Divine Feminine, the monks chanted to the Mother of God. Near the end of the service, when all lights except those above the picture of Our Lady of Guadalupe were extinguished, the sanctuary became the womb of Mary. Monks and retreatants entered a feminine cosmos.

It seemed I had barely fallen asleep when the church bells rang. Shortly after, someone—most likely Brother Mark—shuffled up the eight steps to my door, knocked, and padded away. On the dresser next to my bed, a digital clock read a few minutes before three. Pulling on wool sweaters and slacks, I grabbed a blanket to wrap up in and hurried outside. The air was still and icy; as I followed the boardwalk out to the path, an electric lamp illuminated the small, white breath-clouds I exhaled. Stars shone overhead. At daybreak, when I returned from the zendo, hoarfrost whitened the grass.

After breakfast, I climbed toward the abbey's property line on a high ridge overlooking two wine-producing valleys in the foothills of the Pacific Coast Range. After hiking for nearly an hour, I stopped to catch my breath in a meadow where a small creek ran between deciduous trees, then decided I would not continue the steep climb to the top. That way I would be back for lunch on time, although I would miss seeing the foot-high, white porcelain figure of the Virgin Mary perched on a tree stump, protected from the perpetual Oregon rain by an overturned gallon pickle jar. Instead, later in the week, I would go to an identical Divine Mother shrine across the fields from the monastery where the creeks joined.

Except for an occasional maple displaying late sunny leaves, second growth fir covered most of the abbey's thirteen hundred acres. Among the trees, roads constructed for hauling wood meandered. As I descended the mountain on my favorite path, tiny emerald plants covered the soft ground; treading a royal carpet, occasionally stepping over fresh deer tracks filling with water, I passed yellowing, rust-spotted blackberry vines.

My shoes went pfut, pfut, pfut through dry leaves, squished in boggy hollows, and squeaked on hidden logs. Below the steepest part of the forest, a tiny creek trickled through a meadow, plunged over a leafy brink, and bubbled into the pool below. Occasional birdsong—a tweet tweet tweet, click click, or cascading warble—broke the silence. On my return to the abbey, as I crossed the red brick courtyard, wind sighed in the firs on the hillside above me, and chickadees chattered in the bushes that bordered the path. On the road a quarter mile away, a car engine hummed.

Back in my room, I wrote: *As a child, and later as an adult, the Roman Catholic faith linked me to a history, to a body of people, both living and dead. Each time I attended Mass, the liturgy spoke to me, and I longed for more ... At Ananda, I felt a vibratory connection to the foundation of the universe, and learned to reproduce that deep peace and silence ... Now that I've left the*

*community, I love to be alone, deeply alone, related to All That Is … Perhaps I
do not attain as deep a connection as those with a formal spiritual practice, but
my heart resists discipline, self- or other-imposed. I must be free—silent and free.
I must be who I am.*

*I meditate on what creation looks like. I imagine a stir of white energy, a
reservoir of creativity from which all things emerge, play a brief role, and disappear.
Caught up in daily activity, I'm almost never aware of how fleeting existence
is. Yet, emptiness—the immeasurable "not yet"—the source of all creation—is
Reality, the Self, God, the fertile Mother of all things.*

At lunch, the voice of a monk reading from a new book about Our
Lady of Guadalupe was piped over a speaker from the monastery refectory
to the guest dining room. According to the author, when the Virgin Mary
appeared in 1531 to Juan Diego, she continued the appearances she had
made as the native goddess for centuries before the arrival of the Spaniards.
The disembodied voice of the monk continued, explaining that God and the
Divine Mother—encompassing the entirety of creation—contain both good
and evil. To become whole, Christians must cease polarizing the light and
dark aspects of life.

After stacking my plate and silverware in the dishwasher, I hiked out
the graveled road, past the ponds, to the edge of the forest, then followed a
tiny tributary west through a wooded fairyland. Olive, forest-green, and gray
mosses dangled from bare maple, oak, and alder and covered rocks, stumps,
and fallen logs.

Leaving the creek, I turned south across fallow ground until I came to a
tilled field where puddles reflected the somber sky. Avoiding the wet spots,
I began to cross the area; a third of the way out, my shoes mired in black,
sucking mud. As I pondered my situation, I glanced up at the open sky and
felt myself an insignificant speck on the flat earth—and suddenly, in the
silent immensity, love flooded through me.

*We are loved! Though infinitesimal, we share the creative breath of the Whole.
Subject to the randomness of Being and Not-Being, we are part of all Creation. In
us, the quintessence of Being moves and breathes. With every breath, we participate
in Reality. Intimately bound up in the web of life and not-life, at the heart of each
of us, God breathes, thinks, loves, hates, destroys, and rebuilds—in us! Through
us—in us—consciously and unconsciously, the Divine Mother experiments and
chooses. We—and all creation—advance toward harmony and love. And, on our
journey, Mary, the goddess clothed with the stars and the sun, nurtures us.*

The following morning, after attending Mass, I wrote in my journal:
Near the end of the canon of the Mass, at the culminating moment of consecration,

congregation and priest proclaimed, "Through him, with him, in him, in the unity of the Holy Spirit, all glory and honor is yours, Almighty Father, for ever and ever." Kundalini shivered up my spine.

Simultaneously, I rebel. Why the masculine imagery? Why subordinate the feminine? Despite my admiration of the monks' devotion for Mary, I can never return to a church that refuses to ordain women.

Shortly after midnight, I woke. Whee, whee, whir—tires sang and an engine roared. On the gravel road leading to the forest, urgent male voices—teenagers—shouted directions. Whee, whee, whir. The vehicle broke free. A beam of light streaked across the wall above my bed. The vehicle snarled down the lane and sped into the night. Silence descended. The land murmured.

Somewhat frightened, at least very alert, I wondered, Did they steal my car? Leave a bomb? Envisioning mud and rock flying through the air, I imagined the side of the upper pool rupturing, water flooding into the lower pond. Finally, I fell asleep, only to dream: *The beads on my antique jade necklace pop off. In my hand, I hold five beads. The looser the strand becomes, the easier it will fall apart. Alarmed, I seek out my daughter, who repairs the jewels.* In the dream, fearing the necklace would disintegrate, I turned to the spiritual feminine for assistance. With her dexterous fingers, she strung together the essence of who I am.

Rising early, I meditated, breakfasted in the lodge with other retreatants, and attended Mass. After the service, the hubbub of conversations bubbled and burst in gusts of laughter across the courtyard, breaking my inwardness, propelling me outward.

As I carried books and suitcases to my car, a fat robin and a sleek blue jay argued near the porter's entrance. When I returned for another load, the jay had flown. Perched among sprays of sable seedpods on a dormant shrub, the robin noisily defended her territory. As I turned my car toward the city, I thought, *Just as the Divine Mother will one day return to prominence, the robin prevailed. In the silence of the abbey, I heard her footsteps.*

Red Rock Country

I sat gingerly on the edge of the narrow, leather-covered bench. The white-jacketed chiropractor, a medium-built man with sandy gray hair, stepped into the room.

Generally, a chiropractor will check your posture, ask your symptoms, possibly apply heat pads to relax the muscles, and then adjust your bones to their proper position. This treatment session was different; I was not there for bones to be adjusted, but rather for energetic balancing.

The doctor checked my posture, then touched the nape of my neck and the small of my back. Instructing me to lie face down on the table, he left the room. In a few minutes, he returned, touched my feet, head, and shoulders, and went out again.

As he moved in the hallway from room to room, I heard him answer a patient's question, give a short instruction to another, his voice muffled by multi-chorded music piped through a stereo system. Above the pulsating beat, a clear soprano soared. Soon, a subtle vibration moved in my arms and legs, and up my spine. Fingers and toes tingled; buzzing energy and soulful music blended. The voice sang of marble halls, of love that endured a lifetime.

I left the office, the song playing in my mind. For weeks, as I drove to work, woke from a lazy Saturday afternoon nap, or walked along busy sidewalks—whenever I heard Enya, the Celtic artist, singing—my eyes filled with tears. I bought tapes of her haunting Irish music and played the recordings over and over.

The lyrics evoked the sadness of my childhood. By the time I was seven, Mother had birthed four living children; by my sixteenth year, four more infants had arrived to demand her attention. As Mother's surrogate, caring for younger siblings, I had never had a childhood, never been cuddled or read to. I always longed for love.

At Ananda, I had grown accustomed to the surge of kundalini. Now, in response to the practitioner's gentle touch, the energy moved. When the doctor added his energy to my life force, the kundalini grew stronger. My body moved spontaneously for several minutes; when it stopped, another light touch boosted the power, reinitiating involuntary movement.

Twenty minutes into my third chiropractic treatment, my body tingled from neck to toe, the way an arm or a leg that has gone to sleep feels when it wakes up—a prickling, painful awakening. When I shifted my position on the paper-clad table, the kundalini rushed through blockages in my shoulders. Although I had not performed yoga for four years, not since leaving Ananda, my body arched up in the snake posture. My attention focused on my body's surprising physical responses and I hardly noticed my feelings until after I left the doctor's office. Sitting in my car parked at the curb, a torrent of suppressed grief, feelings trapped in my cells for fifty years, flooded my being; I wept for nameless sorrows.

In another session a few weeks later, the energy moved slowly from the soles of my feet to the crown of my head, tingling the length of my spine, out through my arms, and into my hands. As the life force centered in my pelvis, I twisted and turned, pushing abdominal walls forward, arching my back, stretching hips and thighs. Gradually, the postures changed to the powerful motions of childbirth. I panted and pushed; I seemed to become my daughter, Suzanne, due to deliver her second child that week. Then, I relived the birth of my third child, when, ignoring repeated instructions, hospital nurses had drugged me; Warren was several hours old when I had regained consciousness.

The movement continued. I became my mother birthing eight living children and one stillborn ... I remembered my grandmother Bertha's broad hips and her twenty-year confinement in a wheelchair. Imprisoned in the traditional feminine role until rheumatoid arthritis crippled her, she had served the capricious demands of my old-country grandfather. The face of Hannah, my great-grandmother, appeared ... then Susan, my maternal great-great-grandmother. Focused on the rhythmic breathing and the vibrating energy, I panted, my abdomen expanded; I pushed; a child was born ... I counted seven generations—Susan, Hannah, Bertha, Mary, myself, Suzanne, and my granddaughter Mary.

Weeks later, I attended a daylong "clear out," similar to healing sessions held in hotels across the nation where twenty or more therapists treat five hundred people at once. At the Portland session, while music with a strong beat and beautiful harmony played, fifty men and women "worked" on treatment tables set up in a hotel meeting room. The doctor moved from patient to patient, touching an athletic, sixty-year-old man in the small of the back; a slight, young, blonde woman between the shoulder blades; or a broad-shouldered, middle-aged man behind the knee. The energy in the room built as the hours passed, the healing movement in one patient subtly influencing change in another.

We alternated chiropractic treatments with sound therapy sessions in an adjacent room. Sitting cross-legged on the floor in a circle, we focused our attention on the seven energy centers at the base of the spine, the genitals, abdomen, heart, throat, between the eyes, and at the crown of the head. Toning musical notes, we caused the chakras to vibrate.

Chakras

Seven energy centers located in the etheric body. Located at the base of the spine, the reproduction center, naval, heart, throat, between the eyebrows, and at the crown. Each center has a different spiritual quality. See metaphysical 101 for further information.

Over the next year, new issues surfaced: abandonment, grief, guilt, and rage—loss of self. Taught to suppress my feelings as a small child, I had denied my experience of conflict and pain. A fictitious self—a mask of convention and conformance—sat on the throne of identity, performing acceptable feminine behavior: Defer to men. Be nice, pretty, quiet, polite, and holy. I agreed for the sake of peace, smiled in the face of putdowns, and preferred complacency and passivity to self-expression.

As the chiropractic treatments continued, lifetimes of trapped energy released. Not only suppressed feelings emerged; cellular memories inherited from my ancestors were healed. Increasingly, I felt connected to the feminine and to the numinous original consciousness. Slowly, the pulsating throb of the earth on a still night became the energy of my own body.

One morning as I awoke, a radiant cloud of energy flooded the inner screen of my awareness. Behind my closed eyes, imageless consciousness played. Was this the light of Jesus, or Buddha, God, or Goddess? No, I decided; it was the light of our natural state of being, a pure undifferentiated foundation for all action.

A year after completing the treatments, I dreamed that my chiropractor gave me eight photographs. Each carefully mounted image showed red rock canyon walls and azure blue skies. In the foreground of each picture, trees leafed out with exuberant, new, green growth.

According to Dr. Carl Jung, the Swiss psychotherapist, rocks symbolize the Self. Jung himself had chiseled alchemical messages on the four sides of a perfect twenty-inch cube—his soul stone—placed in the garden of his home in Bollingen, Switzerland. My dream reported that red rocks symbolized my Self, that new growth had begun at the seven energetic centers in my body and at the center above my head. On my 1989 Vision Quest, I had found greenness in a bottlebrush tree. Now spring came to my psyche.

The dream urged me to the American Southwest. I longed to see red rocks and leafing green trees. Six months later, with my friend Maya, I made my first trip to the Navajo reservation. Together, we had decided to attend a three-day Crone Conference in Phoenix; before that, we would spend a week visiting her friends in Sedona, then camping at the Grand Canyon and the Navajo reservation.

In October 1996, at Canyon de Chelly in northeastern Arizona—sacred land of the Navajo people—I hiked the exhilarating twelve-hundred-foot trail from the rim of the canyon to White House, an Anasazi ruin on the valley floor. The ancient, powdery track snaked under, over, and around rocks, sometimes narrowing to a scant two feet in width. Each turn on the trail offered a new perspective—up and downstream, and a mile across the valley floor to a rugged, red stone wall.

I reached White House, a freestanding two-story building adjacent to the north canyon wall, where twenty to forty people once lived in small, interlaced enclosures constructed of red sandstone. I viewed the ruins and then sat in the shade of the cottonwoods, sipping warm water from my canteen, listening to the echoes of a half-dozen tourists' voices, imagining they were the sounds of life in the quiet canyon eight hundred years before. Above the valley, as I looked up between wine-red walls, a lone raptor circled in a turquoise sky. I did not linger—early nightfall and an hour's climb before sunset beckoned me to the rim.

Maya, my traveling companion, met me at the trailhead. We drove east along the rim, climbing higher on the plateau to the road's end. It was dusk when we parked. We hurried down a short trail to a viewpoint overlooking a twenty-mile expanse.

Across the chasm, in burgundy-red walls, tiny Anasazi settlements lodged. A thousand feet below, the light of the setting sun illuminated rivers of red rock talus and glinted on frost-browned grasses. Two tributaries from separate arms of the canyon meandered together, ribbons of water cutting through sand. Downstream, another ancient structure huddled in deepening shadow. In the center of this splendor, Spider Woman—the several-hundred-foot pinnacle sacred to the Navajos—thrust up, piercing the darkening sky.

Night descended into darkness. We returned to the parking lot, our flashlights casting dim circles on the macadam path. As we topped the small rise, radiant bands of sunlight streaked upward from below the horizon fifty miles to the west. A dusky apricot sky shaded upward to cobalt blue, then to velvet blackness where Venus sparkled.

In my mind, Enya's song of marble walls hummed. Canyon de Chelly, the luminescent night, silence, friendship, and Self coalesced in seamless unity. I was home—in myself and in the land—in red rock country.

Sixty-Four to Seventy-Four (1996–2006) Deepening the Divine Feminine
An Ancient Belonging

Outside the Albuquerque terminal, I made a ninety-degree turn. My car skidded on the rain-slicked street. Good grief! I exclaimed. I'm only alone! I'm not ready to die!

I had just dropped my daughter, Suzanne, off for a return flight to California. Now, all at once, the prospect of spending five days by myself two thousand miles from home overwhelmed me. Why? I wondered. I had camped alone for years. Had I grown used to a companion? Was I getting too old?

I quickly assessed my situation—my health was good; I was active and strong; I missed Suzanne, but I would be fine. A night's sleep would do wonders. Still, I thought there was a larger issue—I was searching for a new way of belonging, for a different kind of intimacy.

Glancing at my astrological chart for that period, one can discern long-term trends. Chiron, wounded healer, in the late degrees of Libra, questioned relationships. Pluto, planet of transformation, was in the early degrees of the fourth house of home in Sagittarius; it was approaching the planet ruling learning and communication, changing the things I explored, emphasizing travel and new concepts. Perhaps of most interest, Neptune was engaging with natal Saturn, exploring how solid manifestation and organizations might be spiritualized. Transiting Saturn worked similar energies, applying groundedness to the Moon/Uranus conjunction of my natal chart. Overall, the emphasis seemed to be on spiritualizing the mundane and simultaneously bringing esoteric spiritual ideas into form. Earth and continuity had assumed new importance.

The next morning, when I could delay no longer, I left the sanctuary of the motel and drove north. Speeding toward Santa Fe, I recalled the trip across Nevada on the "lonesomest highway in the world." From lush California, Suzanne and I had driven five hundred miles across barren desert, camped at Island in the Sky and hiked among rock sculptures at Arches National Park. At Canyonlands, above a maze of two-thousand-foot chasms, we had watched cloud shadows move over a ribbon of vegetation bordering the Green River, northwest to the Colorado and south to infinity.

One night, as we set up camp on a treeless bluff in beams of light cast by the car's headlights, Venus glimmered above; constellations appeared through cumulous clouds; and twenty miles away, lightning arced from thunderheads. Four hundred feet below our camp, the San Juan River looped six times in a mile, snaking around granite formations carved out over millennia.

We passed through Monument Valley, Four Corners, and Durango; we viewed pit houses and climbed in ancient Anasazi cliff dwellings at Mesa Verde National Park. And now Suzanne was gone, and I was alone.

After an overnight camp beside the Rio Grande, at Taos Pueblo the following day I joined a tour led by Maria, a shy Native American community college student.

Standing in the center of the wood bridge crossing a small river that divided the plaza, Maria told us, "This pueblo is the oldest city in the country. It's been here a thousand years."

She continued, "Our religion teaches us to keep things natural. We use kerosene lamps; people get their water from the river." Gesturing toward an adobe building topped with a steeple, she said, "Just like you guys, we have holy water in our church." She hesitated, uncertain we would understand, then continued, "The water in the river is holy, too."

Slipping away from the group, I crossed the plaza and entered a quiet, dusky shop. A small native woman looked up from beads she was stringing together, smiled a greeting, and continued her work. I looked around. When I touched a graceful woodcarving depicting an Indian woman, the shopkeeper spoke softly, saying, "The man who carved that is older than either of us."

I imagined a gnarled old man sitting by a wood stove in winter, reminiscing about his bride of seventy years before, as he shaped and polished the wood. Only love and time could create such a fine piece. The sculpture was beautiful, a holy work.

The head tipped back, exposing a strong chin. The eyes were closed, and the open mouth sang. Hair tightly drawn back from the face knotted in a traditional double butterfly; a necklace of tiny white shells circled her neck. She was wrapped in a soft shawl, and a long skirt partially hid her leather leggings and boots. At her feet sat a tiny clay pot patterned in traditional black, beige, and tan. She stood on a lacquered fir base, on which two lines were inscribed in cursive, "Praying for Water, By Alfred L Lujan."

I glanced at the shopkeeper, again at the carving, and ventured, "I'm sixty-four. How old are you?"

The shopkeeper smiled. "Seventy-nine."

"And the artist is older?" Would she tell me more? Who was she? How had she lived?

Ignoring my rudeness, she asked, "Where're you from?"

"Oregon."

I lifted the carving. Varnish hid the fragrance. Close up, the detail was exquisite, each subtle curve and plane carefully delineated; in the soft light cast by wall-mounted kerosene lamps, the statue glowed.

"I was in Oregon once," the shopkeeper said. "I taught at the Chemeketa Indian School in Salem. It's pretty there."

Setting the carving down on the glass case, I moved around the shop; perhaps something less expensive would capture my heart. When I brushed my fingers across a mica-speckled, sable brown pot sitting on a window ledge, the woman whispered, "My daughter made that." She paused, confided, "She put extra shine in the glaze. We're not supposed to do that."

I nodded.

"I'll take the carving," I said. As she took the bills from my hand, her small, brown fingers pressed mine, a silent gesture of intimacy and thanks, acknowledgement of our sisterhood.

She wrapped the carving with attentive care; clearly, it was a holy object, a wise elder's cherished work. She cradled the piece in lightweight beige-brown tissue, wrapped and taped newspaper around it, placed the bundle in a plastic sack, and taped that shut as well.

As she worked, we talked. Was this my first trip to the Southwest? ... I had visited the Hopi Reservation two years before ... Her deceased husband had grown up there.

I hesitated, "My great-great-grandmother was Nez Perce."

Her fingers stilled; her gaze probed my soul. "Are you ashamed?"

"No, no," I stammered. "I don't want to intrude where I'm not welcome."

She nodded understanding and resumed her work.

When the wrapping was complete and the statue placed in a large, brown paper grocery bag, I wanted to prolong my visit. I wished I could think of more to say. Instead, I offered my hand. The woman held it for a moment, looked deep into my eyes, and murmured, "Blessings on your journey." I was touched; she meant my life journey, not the day's drive.

As I drove south along the Rio Grande, the carving tucked safely behind the driver's seat, I tried to imagine how it would be to live in a place like Taos Pueblo for an entire lifetime. Surely, I thought, people who dwell together in the same physical location for a thousand years must have intimacy. They must belong.

Late the following afternoon, in the foothills of the Jemez Mountains, I stopped to read a sign in quiet Bandelier National Monument. Shadows slanted across golden grass; voices echoed between four-hundred-foot canyon walls; a raven flew overhead, its wing feathers whooshing in the azure sky. Sitting on a cottonwood log, I sipped tepid water from my old, olive-green army canteen and considered the climb to the cliff base where ancient dwellers had widened caves into homes in the volcanic tuff.

Since leaving Albuquerque, I had become used to traveling solo. Still, as an older couple passed, I could not help wondering if I would always be alone. Once the most powerful woman in Washington State government, for many years people had turned to stare when I entered a room. Now, invisibility had become my shield. Like millions of older, single women whose children long ago moved out and whose husbands were deceased or divorced, I sought a new way of belonging.

My children told me they loved me, and I knew that they did, but their lives were fast-paced and filled with activity. I tried not to bother them.

A few women friends helped to pass the time. One had integrated every nuance, every tenet of an Eastern philosophy. "No one can tell," she said, "where I leave off and Hinduism begins." Another, devoted to her home and grown children, busied herself with their lives; she had so little free time, she could not meet for a cup of coffee. A third, immersed in a communal building project, had disappeared from my life when she discovered her new purpose.

For a year, I attended a crone's group where we passionately affirmed the beauty, power, and creativity of mature women. We were like the fiery red peppers clustered together, drying in the sun and hanging from rafters in New Mexico roadside shops. Who cared?

In Albuquerque, I met my son Greg, who would accompany me home to Oregon. At our first stop, at El Morro, petroglyphs carved by indigenous people and the writing of latecomer Caucasians sharply contrasted; the first European to reach the area had signed in less than four hundred years before: "Passed by here the Governor Don Juan de Onate, from the Seas of the South on the 16th of April, 1605." I could not help wondering, Is each of us ultimately, truly, related simply to the land, to the continuity of place? Are parents, spouses, children, siblings, co-workers, and casual acquaintances just ephemeral shadows on the walls of time? Mere notes chiseled on our souls?

Greg and I camped on the ancient Anasazi trail to Sedona. We slept one night beneath Ponderosa pines on Grand Canyon's south rim and two nights at the north rim, and stopped beside the Provo and Snake Rivers in Utah and Idaho.

As I lay on firm ground night after night, a connection developed between the earth and me—wholeness wedding me to myself. I felt embraced by the earth. From Oregon to California, to Nevada, Utah, Arizona, and New Mexico, and back, the land rose up to greet me—a five-thousand-mile chorus of nature singing a paean of creation: of high desert, sage and mesquite; pinnacles and peaks, crevices and canyons, valleys, buttes and terraces, plateaus and mesas; of blue and green, pink, purple, gray, white and red rock.

Nature sang the skeletal foundation of the world, the primeval reality of antiquity and duration, of two-billion-year-old layers of rock, of a fifty-thousand-year-old meteor crater, and an ancient, volcanic cauldron. The earth murmured music of walls and faces, precipices and monuments, volcano plugs, and islands in the sky.

I felt the Om song in my body at the center of my being, a melody played in counterpoint to the primal constant. Earth and I existed in intimacy: a harmonious, synchronous unity.

Like the Taos woman who held my hand and blessed me, I belonged. With her, I could say, "On this ancient land, I have walked. I have lived in harmony with the land, the trees, the animals, and the sky. It is good to live in harmony."

Greenfire

In early December 1997, a few weeks after returning home from the Southwest camping trip, I learned that I had won the Walden Fellowship, a six-week writing retreat in Southern Oregon. A grand surprise, I was very pleased with my good fortune. The utility company where I worked as a customer service consultant accommodated my absence with a combined vacation and unpaid leave scheduled for April the following year.

Before I went on the writing retreat, I dreamed: *I enter a dark church. Left of the altar, banks of candles cast flickering shadows on a statue of the Madonna holding the baby, Jesus. To the right of the sanctuary, St. Joseph holds the Christ child in one arm, and in the other arm, he holds a single, long spray of white lilies. A Mass is in progress.*

Making my way across a pew to an empty seat, brushing the heads of people in the row ahead, I murmur, "Excuse me ... pardon me ... I'm sorry." As soon as I sit down, a woman approaches. She asks me to join the celebrant on stage where I am to play the role of an old crone. I rise and totter to the platform.

The priest, a man with warm, brown eyes, greets me. Age has diminished his once robust body, and his shoulders round. He asks, "Will you lead the service?"

In the darkness, I cannot see the print on the page of the lectionary lying open on the pulpit. Am I to start over? Begin where the priest ended? I turn to the white-cassocked man, question him with a lifted eyebrow.

"Begin where you like," he says.

Discarding the semblance of old age, I straighten to full height and begin to read.

Instantly, church and congregation disappear; thousands of worshippers are seated on chairs on the lawn of a sunny outdoor amphitheater.

From a stand of oaks on the right, a plume of smoke rises.

"Fire!" I exclaim.

The priest motions for me to continue.

I speak, and at the sound of my voice, a fifteen-foot-long fissure rips the manicured lawn in front of the platform. Water gushes from the opening. On the surface of the water, green fire dances.

"Run," I exclaim. It's a revolution!"

Carrying a green leather book with a fully open, red rose resting upon it, I race from the stage.

This finest dream I had ever had answered many questions and raised still others. The gloomy, forbidding church had disappeared; in a natural setting, a woman and a man concelebrated a Eucharistic service. Their action seemed positive, yet it precipitated a catastrophic eruption. In the dream, I was frightened. Had the dream woman assumed too much, or was she simply timid after centuries of subjugation?

Even as she cried, "It's a revolution!" she ran. Yet, she carried a rose—symbol of the Divine Feminine—Mary, the Mystical Rose, a familiar figure in Roman Catholicism. Moreover, the rose rested on a green leather book symbolizing a healing message, like the book I was working on.

In April 1998, shortly after the dream occurred, my car rumbled across a plank bridge a few miles north of Gold Hill, Oregon, and climbed half a mile along a narrow lane through fir and madrones. Crossing a myrtle-lined ravine, blue flowers dotting the green groundcover, I rounded a turn and entered a clearing. Below young apple trees, blossoms scattered across a neatly cut lawn.

In the driveway, I greeted Elizabeth Udall, my benefactor for the Walden Fellowship I had won the previous December. Above us, in the pasture above the gravel road, cattle grazed; higher still, wooded hills embraced fields of grass. A hundred feet south, a ten-foot-high deer fence protected Elizabeth's early vegetable garden, and next to the main house, budding wisteria draped a latticed utility shed. From there, a rocked path skirted a flower-bordered goldfish pond and ended a distance beyond at a cedar-shaked, one-room cabin. Below the cabin's single window, purple pansies bloomed in a redwood planter.

Elizabeth gave me a quick tour of the interior of the cabin, and then led me out the back door onto a sundeck that extended from the rear of the cabin across a deep gully. A sloped ramp connected with a madrone-lined path leading to a chicken coop. Next to the ramp, at the end of the charcoal gray deck, a delicate shrub with burnt orange leaves spilled from a massive, brick-red clay pot. On the left side of the deck, doors opened into a bathhouse and a storage room.

After my hostess left, I unloaded the car, arranged my computer and books on a small writing table, and settled a handsome, hand-carved wooden Buddha on a tasseled gold pillow at the back of the dining table. On the windowsill next to the table, a bronze Shiva would dance; fierce Kali, Indian Goddess of discrimination and renunciation, would guard the front entry. On a narrow shelf behind the black, cast iron heater, I placed an ornately painted tin filled with juniper needles from my Vision Quest and my dream journal containing the latest entry, Greenfire Dancing on Water. The full meaning of the dream still eluded me; as I arranged the room, I puzzled about it. Clearly, an inner revolution was underway, and I was to write. Beyond that, I imagined the dream's meaning would slowly unfold.

Taking my journal and a cup of tea, I went out onto the sundeck. Resting in a chair pushed up against the wall of the bathhouse, I sipped tea and wrote for a few minutes, pausing now and then to contemplate my good fortune. Six weeks, I thought, surrounded by nature, with nothing to do but write—an amazing gift!

In the distance, beyond the muted sounds of clucking fowls, water gurgled. South of the deck, above the dry creek bed, one-hundred-fifty-foot locust trees formed a lacy canopy, their pale yellow foliage just budding out. Below the trees, among fragrant purple, white, and plum lilacs, a tiny wrentit flitted. Hearing a flutter above me, I turned in time to see a white-breasted nuthatch settle into the nest in the eaves of the storage room.

A few nights after my arrival, before retiring, I stood in the front doorway enjoying the fresh night air. Above the tree, clouds hid the stars and a waxing full moon. Leaving the door ajar, I crawled into bed, picked up a magazine, and began to read. Moments later, Elizabeth's tawny tabby cat peeked in; when I coaxed her to enter, she skittered away. In my journal, I wrote:

After I found signs of a wild cat on the Vision Quest, images of prowling, sinuous felines captured my imagination. Mystified by my fascination with them and determined to understand it, for nearly a decade I filled the walls of one of my rooms with pictures of tigers, panthers, lions, leopards, and ocelots—cats of every size and description. Eventually, their meaning would be revealed.

Several years passed before I purchased a wall hanging depicting Durga, the Indian goddess, seated sideways on an awesome tiger. From the goddess' head, effulgent rays of light beamed; each of her eight arms held a symbol of enlightenment.

In time, I came to view Goddess and tiger as a single entity, soul and ego united; when I did, the vigilant tiger in me relaxed.

One afternoon, I drove twenty miles to Ashland, a small city at the Oregon-California border noted for its Shakespeare festival. Too late to purchase a ticket to a performance, I settled for *Oscar and Lucinda*, a movie based on the book by award-winning Australian author Peter Carey, at the art film theater. The story relates bringing a glass chapel on a dangerous and difficult journey overland to a remote part of Australia. Once there, the chapel is put aboard a boat, and in the night, she sinks.

That night, in a dream, an Irishman spoke: *One wonders how we've done it, me father and me, and me two wee brothers. We've brought the pianer across by boat, in the inky black night, on the dark rolling waves, we have. Strapped to the boat she was, her legs hanging free. And we done it. We brang home this fine playing machine, with her great value, and her great beauty. We floated her in, and lifted her ashore, with nary a scratch to show, her wires all dry and shining in the sun.*

I imagined I was the piano safely ashore after a wild ride on a tumultuous sea.

One morning at daybreak, pelting rain, driven by gusts of wind, woke me. Crashing on the roof, the clatter climaxed in torrential waves of sound. A sheet of sleet-gray water pounded the pasture, beat the leafing raspberry canes, and soaked the lawn. In front of the cabin, fog enveloped the sun locust, delineating moss-covered dead limbs jutting out among live branches; white light poured through the pane. As the storm passed, water plunked in puddles, whispered on limbs, dripped from branches, sighed off eaves, and trilled down spouts. Outside the north window, a bird chirped. Across the pasture, above the farm manager's house, an owl hooted.

In my journal, I wrote: *I am developing a personal theology of God within, dispensing with gurus and institutions. I experiment with teachings and practices and choose from among them; ultimately, I live from my values, not according to collective opinion.*

As long as I followed religious authorities, my spirituality and psyche remained separate. Now, the more inward I become, the less separation I feel; body, mind, and soul are becoming a continuum.

The Self, the creative feminine, reaches beyond the rational. In dreams, hunches, and synchronicity, I have learned to recognize the creative intelligence that embraces us—in which we live—an ebbing, cresting sea of knowledge.

For at least fifteen years, I have suspected that the Self, not my personal ego, determines the pattern of my life. After I left the governor's office, she decided I would not find work until I became a campus minister and attended seminary. Four years later, she prompted the move to Ananda. Then, after I visited the Shiva temple in Kashmir, the disparity between my Self-knowing and the role I played clashed. Ultimately, the difference between my soul and my ego, between who I am and what I believed others thought I should be, catapulted me out of the ashram.

I first became aware of the interlacing of life, the vast realm of the Self, when Greg, then a five-month old baby, had pneumonia and nearly died. Sensing an eight-foot angel hovering behind me, protective wings spread wide, I thought I was losing my mind. During the week Greg was hospitalized, the angel accompanied me. Years later, on the Vision Quest, I felt the same presence. After the Ananda reprimand, when I did not know what I would do, a suffused network of energy—Carl Jung's collective unconscious—sustained me.

Others describe this context of life—this Reality—as God, Truth, Beauty, Love, and Light. Lately, I experience Reality as simple belonging, as comforting as a warm bath or one's bed after a tiring day. No matter what occurs, a loving, supportive Presence sustains me.

And now I see the aliveness; consciousness permeates every niche and cranny of the universe: what I need comes to me. My life is a part of the whole, the expression through the rational "me" of ideas waiting to be felt and lived. I need not accumulate, strive, hurry, force, or worry; I need only accept the unfolding of life. Resting in the core of my being constitutes the sum of all I must do.

In the fourth week of my six weeks at Walden Farm, Garth, my old student friend who introduced me to Ananda, visited. Throughout the five days of his visit, his presence—what he was doing, what we would do together, and when—inhibited me. My writing would begin to flow, then I would interrupt it to check with him: was this, or that, what he wanted?

After he left, I returned to my deep self, questions rippling through my mind like the wake of a small boat on a placid lake. I had been enamored of this man's beauty, his speech, writing, storytelling, and meditation practice for years; once, he was the most spiritual person I knew. The dream of Greenfire suggested I had made progress in integrating my inner masculine and feminine qualities. Certainly, I no longer looked to my young friend for direction. As the clouds of his visit dissipated, I tried to understand our differences. How had I changed?

I wrote: *Since leaving Ananda, I experience fewer peaks and valleys. One insight has led to another. Network Chiropractic released physical blocks in my body, some of them inherited in ancestral genes. At The Forum, a yearlong process of discernment, I explored childhood abandonment. After attending a counseling group for six months, I discarded the immature masculine part of myself who enticed me with spiritual transcendence.*

When my childhood abandonment issues resurfaced, I spoke with a spiritual counselor. I told her that I had thought that I had come to terms with those old concerns—that Mother had done the best she could, had loved me, and had never been the all-powerful figure every child believes her parent to be.

Watching my children and the children of my siblings and friends enter mature adulthood, observing their mistakes and celebrating their successes, I had concluded that we had done the best we could—as had our parents. Although the abandonment—the inconsolable loss I felt as an infant—had repeated when I was nine after I skipped a grade, and again at Ananda, both experiences brought me closer to self-understanding. I resigned myself to living with my loss.

"Let's look at that resignation," the spiritual counselor suggested.

"There's a black hole in the center of my heart. I can't go there!" I told her.

"Just this one time, I'll go with you," she replied.

I imagined myself as a three-year-old child holding the hand of an older, blonde girl with braids. Shaking with terror, I entered the void.

Instantly, the awful emptiness disappeared; I was alone in a star-filled sky. I felt secure, completely at peace.

The moon eclipsed the sun; from the concealed surface of the great round light, crescendos of energy burst and shimmered.

Stars, moon, and sun disappeared.

I stood in a subtly tinted, soft, billowing cloud—in enveloping potentiality, the stuff of life: in primeval consciousness.

Abandonment yielded to creativity.

I have never lost the sense of peace I felt in that moment. I had reached the end of my long search. After nearly sixty years, the mystery of my being had resolved. The ache was gone. After so much inner work, at last I had the courage to step across the forbidding black chasm at the center of my heart.

Perhaps, as Garth said, I was too inward and too intense, but I could not respond in any other way. Before Kali and her sword of discrimination graced my life, I had thought transcendence was the ultimate spiritual goal. Now, after several years of exploring the Divine Feminine, willing myself to perfection seemed an escape from nature, from simple living, a denigration of the ordinary.

In the writing cabin, peace and stillness sustained me. I enjoyed a slower rhythm, mice in the walls, cackling chickens in the pen, a fire in need of tending. The homey sound of a shifting log broke the quiet; the stove gently ticked, and the fire fluttered. From the writing retreat, I returned to a new home west of Mount Hood in the foothills of Oregon's Cascade Mountains. Outside my window, old growth cedar frame my view of a duck pond dappled in sunlight. Birds twerp and tweet, chirp and chatter. A squirrel scampers up a tree. I have no need for a transcendent God.

Jesus preached, "The Kingdom of God is within"; Yogananda taught, "Silence is the altar of God." The truth—of who I am, of whomever each of us is—derives from Spaciousness and Silence—from the Self within.

In The Garden of a Dream Hotel

I first had the recurring dream when I was seven. I was attempting to cross the road near my home to catch the school bus. A long line of cars traveled bumper to bumper, sped up, slowed down and separated, to prevent me from crossing. No matter what I tried, I could not cross.

As I grew, the line of vehicles became a railroad train. In my thirties, I dreamed I was too large to slip down the smokestack of a steam engine; in another dream, a train ricocheted at high speed along a narrow-gauge track in the Swiss Alps.

Now, I dreamed that a toy engine pulling little, red cars careened around the perimeter of a hotel garden. As the locomotive and boxcars circled the resort's seating area, I knelt under the waist-high track and watched the earth rotate, one fir tree after another passing through my line of vision. From a little girl's shifting identities that obstructed her passage, my perspective had expanded to an evolving planetary view.

Identity, I have learned, is as illusory as early morning sunshine on a wind-riffled pond. In response to fleeting experience, emotions play out: happy, sad, bored, angry, peaceful, conflicted, lonely, or joyful. "I" is a shifting phenomenon, a passing dream. Like Shiva Nataraj, the supreme God of Hindus, life dances. Once I was a student, then a mother anticipating a child's birth, later a feminist politician, and still later, a spiritual seeker.

Slowly, I learned to live this ephemerality, establishing routines, creating order, living this way, then that. I became the time, the place, the person I was with. I had no identity; I had all identities. I became energy flowing, endlessly forming, disappearing and reappearing. Who I am became a perspective, a belief system, a skeletal icosahedron suspended in a vast, cloudless sky. If I changed my belief, I changed myself.

For much of my life, I longed for a mystical connection with something or someone greater than myself. I first found that union in the Communion wafer, later in ecstatic tongue-speaking. In the seventies, I found God in the mysticism of Buddhism, Hinduism, and Judaism, and in the beliefs of Muslims, Celts, and Amerindians. In the eighties, I found communion in the movement of the breath inward and outward, in the flow of kundalini energy in my spine.

In the nineties, I found the Divine Feminine in my mother, in myself. In the last decade, I have found the Divine in nature, in the stars in a night sky, in the ceaseless sound of the sea. I found the Divine Mystery in antiquity, in longevity, in ancestry and in ancient peoples, in red rocks and high mountains, in trees and great flying birds, and in the bedrock of the earth.

Most significantly, after a lifetime of searching, I found God within my Self. Now, having lived a woman's story, I speak for freedom for every soul, for union with the divine Self within, for co-creation and co-inherence—I in God; God in me—for the divine dance.

Paramahansa Yogananda, the teacher I followed for many years, sang, "I am a bubble; make me the sea." "I" is the soul; the soul is a drop in the sea of God. Dancing in the soul, one depends on the ocean—waves cresting here, now there, endlessly shifting, swirling, and turning on the sands of time. Existence is a playground where we learn to accept our own and others' foibles and eventually become dancing gods. Then, happiness spills over in a kaleidoscope of shapes and colors, a rollicking foot-stomping romp.

When I am not dancing, I love Silence, the source of all things. I love the space without sound, without words, lines, boundary, or form. Out of Silence arises the primal first sound, Om, proclaiming the infinity of exploding/ imploding energy. From Silence, from the creative, feminine womb of the cosmos—all energies, all consciousness, all thoughts, all things spill in and out of creation. Silence—mother of all things—births clouds, butterflies, squalling babies, planets, trees, and raindrops—and enfolds them once again when their cycle ends.

Because I love the creative sound of Om, its Sanskrit ideograph, ॐ, hand woven into a black and ivory wool tapestry, hangs above my altar, a perpetual reminder of my ephemeral self, of my oneness with all things.

Reflecting on the most difficult time of my life, after my shattering encounter with the Goddess Kali, years passed before I attained tranquility. Yet, the dark night of the soul I endured led to the emergence of my true Self—for which I was born.

What kept me going? Courage? Perhaps. Mostly, I simply would not, could not, give up. The imperative I heard at eight—not willfulness, nor vanity, nor personal desire—demanded I follow my inner impulse. If I did not, I would not complete the task for which I had been born. I would not become who I was meant to be.

ॐ

Jungian analyst Irene Claremont de Castillejo concluded her 1973 book, *Knowing Woman, A Feminine Psychology*, with a dream in which she descended deep into the earth and reemerged carrying an exhausted, bewildered woman, symbol of the repressed feminine. Ms. de Castillejo wrote, "… (I) appeal to all of those of you who feel the task worthwhile, to help lift this figure, which I believe to be the image of the feminine soul of woman, right up into the sunshine and lag her on the green, growing grass of conscious reality." Her plea made an enormous impact on me, so such so that I decided to find my own feminine self, and, if possible, to share the journey with others.

The archetypal dream of Greenfire erupting from the earth is a response to Ms. de Castillejo's appeal. The dream points to a revolution in consciousness, to a time when every person, embodying masculine and feminine qualities, will become an integrated, conscious agent, creatively living her or his unique calling. Affirming God within each person, the coalescing of ego and Self, the marriage of rational, cognitive thought with intuitive, preconscious awareness, the dream builds upon the message I heard at Sri Yukteswar's Samadhi Mandir in India: "All your cares, all your worries, all your sorrow, never really happened." When the personality disappears, when one unites with *Sat-chit-ananda* (Pure, Unchanging, Bliss)—with the timeless Self, with the Divine Feminine—pain does not exist.

The dream announced that the Absolute underpins individual consciousness, that the Self supports the personality. Eternal Reality, the foundation of life, provides the lustrous setting in which everything—pain, joy, and love—dances and shimmers. From the hidden recesses of age-old religion, the clear light of consciousness illuminates a new spiritual path.

The Divine Feminine, the energy of wisdom and compassion, permeates the world. She is the power of the universe, she who creates. She is Shakti, Shekina, Sophia, Kundalini, Durga, Kali, White Buffalo Woman, Tara, Mary, Inanna, and Isis. One morning several years ago, she danced onto my paper:

I am the creative life force. I am strength, creation, consciousness, love, compassion, joy, and peace. I am authentic self-expression. I am the power of the universe, the wind on the mountain, and the foundations under the sea. I am the gut-wrenching power that flows through your pen, the power that holds your heart wide open, pouring out love in a fiery stream.

I love you: my life, my people. My heart is a volcano from which red-hot lava flows, a rush of energy from the center of the earth, an ocean of tenderness. My heart is a fountain, a white torrent arching over, gushing five hundred gallons a minute. My heart is full: full of the world, full of the people.

I love all those who fight for justice and freedom. The voices of today combine with the music of twenty thousand years ago, with the song of pioneers marching across the wilds of the globe, riding a wave of life, of future, of possibility. Living, dying, loving, healing, surviving, enduring, determined to be, to discover, to create. Inflamed by the power of life itself—onward, onward, never stopping—a mighty shout.

You cannot compromise. You cannot accept things the way they are simply because they have always been. Examine for yourself. Choose what is valid. Be yourself. Follow your heart. Act from necessity, one with the onward sweep of history, a creative partner with All That Is.

In 1989, I placed a healing crystal atop a barren desert ridge and pledged to become a transformer, to draw down Reality. I imagined that, for all time, to every point on a 360-degree circle, healing would radiate out from the crystal to every person on the earth. Today, the metaphor from the old hierarchical model, drawing down Reality, no longer serves.

My life experiences have transported me to a wordless domain, to the deep feminine, not to the heavens. In time, the mantra I adopted, "Who am I?" confirmed a spacious emptiness/fullness, a consciousness where all creation is interdependent, where nothing exists in isolation.

Today, I view myself as a "two-phase" person. One aspect of me, the personality, delights in the stories of my ancestors, remembers my past, engages in daily activity, and dreams of accomplishment. The other aspect—the Soul-Self I heard for the first time at eight, glimpsed as a twenty-year-old, and merged with over the years—the source of the healing that flows through me, arises out of—is—Shakti, the Eternal Feminine.

Reality exists in—and only in—this very moment. In this present moment, now, I recall the past; *from this present moment, from the now,* I project the future. *Now,* I commit myself to witness and to participate, to join with every living person, with every living being, with all creation.

The sadness I knew as a child is gone. I am at home in my deepest Self—content in the Eternal Feminine, in harmony with All That Is.

THE PRESENT (2007–2008)
SACRED MARRIAGE AND BEYOND

I was surprised to discover how life settled down after my son Greg and I moved to our home east of Portland, a place I've named Kailasha in honor of the mythical abode of Shiva, the transcendent Indian god.

In 1999, my mother entered a foster home after having a stroke. I visited there often until her death in 2004. Her last years were peaceful; our visits were laughter-filled, a time of joy. At her request, at her funeral in a Catholic church in southern Washington State, I was privileged to read a letter I had written to her, celebrating her life accomplishments.

Until early 2006, I worked part time at a regional utility, developed a small business, and took writing classes at Lewis and Clark College and Marylhurst University. I retired to complete my spiritual memoir and to devote more time to my astrological business.

A blessing these last ten years has been the gift of my youngest son's presence in my life. Like me, he thrives on metaphysical and spiritual matters. Greg is my companion, practicing, I sometimes tell him, for when I enter advanced old age. Among my acquaintances, no one shares the same interests and spiritual insights as he and I together. His illness—very likely the result of the early childhood respiratory difficulty from which he barely survived—is a gift to both of us, an opportunity to learn compassion and patience, a learning that will serve him well in the future.

Ever since the police found Greg lost and confused in the city and contacted me, I have known of our karmic connection. Key planets in his chart, Pluto and Uranus, the ones responsible for his temporary confusion, sit astride my ascendant. I have great empathy for women who love and care for children with incurable chronic illness. They are the unsung heroines of our time.

My son's emotional ups and downs forced me to take one tiny step and then another, to find new ways of cheering him when he was despondent, new approaches to celebrating increments of growth. How vividly I remember Christmas Eve 1991, the day I read an article stating the condition he shares with millions of others would never worsen from what it was five years after onset.

We have enjoyed Christmases with my sister, Lucille, and her husband, Ron, in their lovely southwestern Washington home on many occasions, with numerous cousins, aunts and uncles, children and grandchildren present. We have driven to California for a celebration with my daughter and her family. We have had quieter Christmases at home with my sons Paul and Warren and their spouses. But the one that stands out is a simple meal at a landmark Chinese restaurant in east Portland. Not a particularly festive Western Christmas with tree and decorations, but one where I knew for the first time that my son's health would never deteriorate and would likely improve. What a Christmas celebration that was!

In 1998, Greg completed his bachelor's degree in interdisciplinary studies at Marylhurst University. He was employed by a credit card bank for eight years before beginning a helping career.

At a seminar I attended in the fall of 2004, the founder of Shamanic Astrology, Daniel Giamario, spoke about spirituality, dreams, mythology, psychology, archetypes, astrology, archeology, ancient peoples, and more. Nothing I had experienced for years enchanted me as much as his lecture. When I learned that he had developed an apprentice program, I questioned how I could justify the expenditure of several thousand dollars from my retirement fund to take his courses.

Shamanic Astrology

A school of astrology based on material sourced by Daniel Giamario. Shamanic astrology emphasizes the degree of the sky on the eastern horizon (the Ascendant), the Moon and its nodes, at the time of birth. The school is experiential, paying attention to the actual position of the planets in the sky at any given time, together with the changing positions of planets within their regular cycles. Drawing on mythology, psychology, philosophy, and astroarchaeology, shamanic astrologers ascertain the life intent of the individual together with the challenges and gifts one brought into life at birth. For more information, see shamanicastrology.com.

That fall, during the ninth return of Venus to the place in the sky where it had been at my birth, Greg and I traveled to the Yucatan Peninsula to visit Mayan archeological sites. I felt particularly blessed to greet Venus at Palenque that day, at the site where King Pacal had flourished and died a millennium ago.

In early 2005, "Follow your bliss," won out. I traveled to New Mexico, Arizona, Nevada, and in Oregon over the next year, studying both advanced astrology and the night sky from remote mountaintops. In November 2005, under a Venus Moon conjunction, I became a certified shamanic astrologer. The graduation ceremony took place at the center of a one-hundred-foot stone circle aligned to the changing sky, on a hilltop in the south-central New Mexico desert. Since then, as so often happens under a Venus return cycle, my spiritual counseling practice expanded.

In mid-May 2007, I attended a shamanic astrology event centered on the theme of sacred marriage and relationship. Combining breathwork and astrology, the leaders, Kate McKee and Daniel Giamario, accompanied each participant on an inner journey and then related the experience to the person's astrological chart.

Nurtured by the Divine Mother in sacred space, at a retreat located on a bluff overlooking the ocean where Indian women held healing ceremonies for hundreds of years, I had imagined that my first breathwork would be a journey into a world of images. Instead, I stayed steadily aware of energy moving in my spine. No animal guides came to accompany me. Rather, I felt the loving presence of my mother, who had died three years before; my soul Self—a larger-than-life-size woman in white; and Babaji, whom I associate with the Unmanifest God, Shiva.

Breathing to the rhythm of a strong musical beat, in a few minutes my body began to perform yoga postures. About twenty minutes into the breathwork (time lost all meaning) my arms began tracing pentagrams in the air above me. The five-sided figures felt too complex, so I simplified to a diamond similar to those I had been weaving in a Navajo tapestry for the past year. *Diamond consciousness*, I thought, *diamond clarity*. Over and over. *Diamond consciousness, diamond clarity.*

When I heard odd noises in the room, I became amused, laughing quietly until another woman guffawed, and I joined her. Life is so funny! I thought.

Now, the energy was in the first chakra and concerned the abandonment I felt as an infant. But instead of feeling sorry for myself, I cried for my mother. Mother and departed family members were with me, pleased I was doing this work. It seemed that, rather than having been abandoned as I had felt for so many years, I had abandoned myself before I came into this life.

I began working at the third eye and then at the crown chakra, remembering the meditations twenty years before at Puri, India, at Sri Yukteswar's Samadhi Mandir, and at the temple above Srinagar where Shiva accepted my self-offering. Babaji-Shiva is with me, I thought, remembering how I wept inconsolably for hours, remembering the voice that told me, "All your cares, all your sorrows, never really happened."

ॐ

And I knew, the breathwork confirmed, that in the body, in duality, we experience pain, but in the world of Being, of Unity Awareness, nothing is happening, has ever happened.

As I breathed, energy streamed through me, clearing the crown chakra, bringing in new energy from outside the body.

When I stopped weeping for the pain and sorrow we experience in duality consciousness, in my mind I yelled at (masculine) Spirit/God/guide, *"You promised me enlightenment ..."* and understood that I had been given it. Everything I experienced during the breathwork seemed connected to the message I had heard when I was eight, telling me I had a mission. Several times, a voice repeated, *"You are my Beloved in whom I am well pleased."*

Again and again I returned to, "All your cares, all your sorrows, never really happened," and I wept for the suffering that had been, that continues in the world of duality. Simultaneously, I knew: everything in this world is simply God's play—lila; simultaneously, I laughed for joy and cried for universal sadness and sorrow.

During a tiny space of quiet, I asked, "I want clarity of mission—how do I share wisdom?... The answer: laughter/joy.

That night I worried about how to present the story of my journey. It would sound so inflated. By morning, it was clear. I wrote in my journal: *Just as the mystical core of all religions is the same, so is the source of individual worldviews. All is from the same source! Truth is the life force/chi/kundalini/ energy in all things and in each of us. Using this energy, we each build different paradigms. Just as this energy informs every chakra, it is in every thing, down to dirt and rocks and space. Because it is in all things, saints see themselves and the world as one.*

The next day, with stacks of magazines scattered over the floor, we spent hours finding pictures to reflect our shamanic journeys. As we worked on the vision boards, I realized that my inner marriage combined the energy of Mars and Pisces in my astrological chart. A longtime friend embodies the King figure and another friend, the Piscean figure. Still, it had always been my own energy projected onto them; now I claimed it as my own.

I found pictures of mature and powerful men, brilliant and creative people, and an array of spiritual images to place on a field of fiery red. A workshop leader summed up the archetype: Leo/Pisces in service to humanity. Economist, musician, media star, politician, poet, actor. All empathic to people and the earth, deeply connected to nature. My inner beloved is powerful, intuitive, spiritual, conscious, making a difference in the world, aware, in love with silence, compassionate and caring.

ॐ

Crossing the Columbia River from Oregon to Washington a week after the breathwork, I suddenly knew that the voice I heard when I was eight years old was actually the combination of Mars in Leo and my seventh house descendent in Pisces … the archetype of service to the earth and its people. I had devoted my life to learning what I finally integrated at the workshop.

A month later at a follow-up conference on the astrology of relationships and sacred marriage, I was reminded that my soul requires a container—a body. It's fun to soar in spiritual skies, but Spirit was telling me to live with the nitty-gritty of life, to integrate the two.

After another Venus/Moon ceremony that evening on the same beach we had been at four weeks before, I walked back to my room, humming a silly tune, "Hello, my baby; hello, my honey; hello, my ragtime doll." At the same time, tears welled up—I was alone at dusk on a sandy beach in my no longer agile body. Joy and tears. Tears and joy. Both at the same time. I thought, *It's all God's play, all lila.*

A week later, at a group Zen meditation, spiritual energy filled my abdomen, suggesting that the goal is to integrate spirit and body. Ultimate consciousness, non-dual awareness, is simultaneously aware of both duality and non-duality. It's not a question of one or the other; it's both at the same time—sadness as you walk alone, joy for the beauty of it all.

I am ready for new learning. Beyond is an abiding experience, not simply an intellectual knowing that all is lila, God's play. We are indeed the two-phased creatures I intimated in the mid-nineties.

And my life mission? I'm still discovering. One contemporary teacher of non-duality believes that our level of consciousness affects everyone around us; the clearer we become, the more we enable others. Perhaps, after a lifelong search, this was my purpose.

If so, I invite you to join me in the effort to become more conscious, to discover the myriad ways soul continually operates in *your* life—to be more at home in the Divine, more conscious of the Soul, more in love with the Self, at One with Nature and with All Beings. Together we can make this world a paradise.

Blessings and love,
Jo Mills Garceau

PART TWO

Metaphysics 101 for the Knowing Woman

ANANDA SPIRITUAL COMMUNITY

An intentional spiritual community founded by Donald Walters (Swami Kriyananda) in 1968 in the foothills of the Sierra Nevada in north-central California. The community now has centers in several United States cities, India, and Italy.

ASTROLOGY—BASIC PLANETS, HOUSES, SIGNS AND THEIR INFLUENCES

An ancient system of viewing the skies, attributing influences of the stars and planets on humanity and earth events. The philosophical basis of astrology is "As Above, So Below." The 360-degree arc of the sky is divided into twelve segments, called houses. Originally, houses were congruent with specific constellations. The houses retain their names, but the Earth's orbit and tilt results in a one-degree change relative to the sky every seventy-two years (called "precession"). Thus, houses and constellations have become somewhat different over time.

Planets and their general influence:

Sun – The engine that drives all planetary energies
Moon – Nurturing, parenting, moods
Mercury – Communication, restlessness
Venus – Love, values, money
Mars – Action, martial arts, conflict, energetic
Saturn – Boundaries, limitations, organization, structure
Jupiter – Expansion, good fortune, freedom, travel in the mind and physically
Uranus – Sudden insight, pioneering, abrupt change
Neptune – Expanded consciousness, confusion, spirituality, drugs
Pluto – Change, transformation, manipulation, power

Signs and their general influence:

Aries – Ruled by Mars, a fire sign, beginnings, energy, conflict
Taurus – Ruled by Venus, an earth sign, the physical plane, sensuality
Gemini – Ruled by Mercury, an air sign, communication
Cancer – Ruled by Moon, a water sign, nurturance, parenting

Leo – Ruled by Sun, a fire sign, self-confidence, rulership, world server

Virgo – Ruled by Mercury, an earth sign, health professions, discrimination and detail

Libra – Ruled by Venus, an air sign, love and relationships

Scorpio – Ruled by Pluto, a water sign, intense and passionate, transformation

Sagittarius – Ruled by Jupiter, a fire sign, explorer, traveler, learner, expansion

Capricorn – Ruled by Saturn, an earth sign, organizations, management, structure

Aquarius – Ruled by Uranus, an air sign, pioneering, intellect, thinker, avant-garde

Pisces – Ruled by Neptune, a water sign, collective unconsciousness, spiritual

Houses and their general import:

First – Personality, how others see you, life intent

Second – Values, income

Third – Neighborhood, siblings, communication

Fourth – Home

Fifth – Creativity, lovers, romance, children

Sixth – Health, work (especially with the hands)

Seventh – Others, partnerships

Eighth – Other people's money, change and transformation

Ninth – Higher education, travel, religion, philosophy, psychology

Tenth – Career, profession, manner of giving to the collective

Eleventh – Groups, organizations, friends

Twelfth – Hidden aspects, collective unconscious, institutions and hospitals

CATHOLIC CHARISMATIC MOVEMENT

A Pentecostal Movement among conventional Christians, especially Catholics, of the early 1970s, which began at Notre Dame University and spread across the country. Based on the concept that the Holy Spirit, the Spirit of God, can be active in lay men and women.

CATHOLIC SYMBOLS AND RITUALS

Baptism – Immersion in water, or sprinkling by water, in a ritual that welcomes a newborn (or an adult just entering the church) into the body of believers, the church community.

Holy Communion – A sacrament wherein one eats and drinks consecrated bread and wine, not symbolic but, according to church doctrine, the living body and blood of Jesus Christ.

Confession/Reconciliation – A sacrament wherein one confesses one's sins, which are then absolved.

CHAKRAS

The seven etheric centers in the human body are located along the spine as noted below. Each has a particular energy, also listed below.

1. Base Chakra – base of spine – strength and endurance
2. Reproductive Center – creative
3. Navel Center – ambition and power
4. Heart Center – love
5. Throat Center – speech
6. Third Eye Center – mental
7. Crown – spiritual

CRYSTALS AND OTHER GEMSTONES

Products of the earth, these natural formations carry different energies and are often used to heal or to change one's vibration. There are literally hundreds of them; any good metaphysical store will carry several books on the stones and their qualities. Some of the more popular ones with their attributes are listed below:

Quartz – used for clarity and meditation

Rose Quartz – used for the giving and receiving of universal unconditional love

Obsidian – used for absorbing negative energy

Snowflake Obsidian – used for meditating on the patterns/disconnections/connections in your life

Apache Tears – used for working through grief

Amethyst – used for peace, harmony, and working through addictions

Malachite – used for health

Citrine – used for dispelling nightmares, enhancing creativity

GODDESSES AND GODS

Cernunnos – a Welsh chthonic father-god, consort to Cerridwen

Cerridwen – a Welsh chthonic mother-goddess with three faces (maiden, mother, and crone)

Kali – the supreme goddess of discrimination, associated with death and transformation

Shiva – One of the high gods of India, in Kashmir the Unmanifest Ultimate God Consciousness

Shakti – The feminine spiritual energy inhabiting all things

Note: Shiva and Shakti are so intertwined, one cannot speak of one without the other.

I CHING

An ancient Chinese oracle. Originally small sticks were thrown, and the manner in which they fell determined the seeker's fortune. There are sixty-four hexagrams, each made up of six lines, based on eight trigrams reflecting natural symbols. Moving lines result in constant change in the outcome of throws.

JUNGIAN PSYCHOLOGY

Pioneer in transpersonal psychology, C. G. Jung was the first to suggest the human personality extends beyond the physical body. Following are some major themes developed and reported on in Jung's voluminous writings over a period of more than fifty years.

Dreams – Jung studied dreams extensively and developed them with his patients as a means of entering the personal and collective unconscious.

Collective Unconscious – Jung posited a now generally accepted concept that a realm of conscious awareness beyond individual consciousness can be accessed. The collective unconscious draws from the individual unconscious of everyone who has lived or now lives, but is vastly larger than the totality of individuals, extending deep into the human past and to the farthest reaches of spiritual awareness.

Anima – The feminine in a man, his soul figure.

Animus – The masculine in a woman who speaks on her behalf, but is not her soul.

Archetypes – In the collective unconscious are numerous symbolic energies common to all humanity. Individuals unconsciously draw upon these models as patterns of behavior. Shamanic astrology uses these extensively, correlating them to planetary energies, for example.

Typology of Personality – Jung developed a typology based on four spectrums of human thought and behavior. For each of the four, an individual will place somewhere on the spectrum (i.e., from very introverted to very extroverted, and so forth). Utilizing the four categories immediately below, one might be an INFP (Introverted Intuitive Feeling Perceiver), which the author is, or one might be (randomly chosen) an ESTJ (Extroverted Sensate Thinker Judge). These personalities, both normal and found in any collection of individuals, will act in quite different ways. In fact, they may find themselves quite at odds depending on where they rest on their respective spectrums. Churches and business organizations have found it helpful to know the typology of people that make up their constituency. Different people work better together than others, make better marriage partners, and so forth.

- Introvert/Extrovert – The spectrum concerned with whether one thinks before speaking (introvert), or speaks in order to know what one is thinking (extrovert).

- Intuitive/Sensate – The spectrum of awareness, extending from a deep, intuitive knowing on the one hand, to a solid grasp of the five senses on the other.

- Thinker/Feeler – A spectrum moving from a logical model of how things are on the one hand, to a feeling about how things are on the other. A thinker works with ideas; a feeler with feelings.

- Judge/Perceiver – A "judge" weighs everything against his/her internal model. A "perceiver" weighs all issues according to a felt perception.

Synchronicity – Jung wrote extensively about a phenomenon where a seemingly unrelated thing will have singular impact on another. The most famous example involved a counselee who had dreamed of an Egyptian beetle. As Jung and the woman talked about the dream, a beetle of this sort, never found in the area before, flew in the window. The impact on the woman was so profound that her self-awareness changed, leading to a resolution of a deep-seated problem.

Ego and Self – Jung posited a model of consciousness where the personality presented to the world is a portion of the conscious ego, the little self. The totality of the individual, the Self, is much greater, but is not known to the ego. Therapy, dreams, and meditation are tools that loosen egoic boundaries, permitting increasing Self-awareness.

Mandala – Generally based on circular forms, Jung wrote about and used mandalas extensively as symbols of wholeness, unity, the Self.

Kundalini, Chi, Life Force

In Indian spiritual lore, Kundalini is a feminine goddess of energy—Shakti—that inhabits all living things. Known throughout the world by many names, the life force informs all creation. Kundalini, when freed, runs in the central channel of the etheric body, called the sushumna. To the left and right of this conduit reside the ida and the pingala. The caduceus is a representation depicting the ida and the pingala winding around the sushumna.

Mantra

Words repeated by a spiritual devotee, they are considered to be the energy of the god or goddess whose name is intoned. One of the most famous is Om Mani Padme Hum, murmured all over the world as a way of centering in the heart of the lotus, the spiritual center. In Christianity, repeated phrases such as Jesus, Mary, Joseph, or Lord Jesus, have mercy on me, a poor sinner, are a form of mantra.

MOON PHASES

As it circles the Earth on its monthly rotation, the moon goes through repeating phases. We are all familiar with the dark of the moon, the new moon, the full moon, and the quarter moons. Depending on the phase of the moon under which a person (or a project begun) is born, different attributes and tendencies will manifest.

SEERS, MEDIUMS, READERS

Individuals whose intuitive skills are highly developed. Some see with their inner eye, others travel into alternative realities. Many intuitives use a tool, such as a deck of tarot cards, the I Ching, or an astrological wheel as a starting point. As they work with a client, insights come to them.

SELF

The part of an individual reflecting her or his essence. There is a little self, or ego, and a Higher Self that is capable—with focus, determination, prayer, and meditation—to become one with the Totality of all creation.

SHAMANIC ASTROLOGY

An experiential system of astrology sourced by Daniel Giamario, based on the actual movement of heavenly bodies in the night sky. Emphasis is on location of the moon and the eastern horizon at the time of birth. The moon indicates the intent of the previous lifetime and those qualities brought forth to the new life. The ascendant, the point at the eastern horizon at the time of birth, shows the present life intent. All references to charts and astrology in *Knowing Woman* Part I are based on the Shamanic Astrology Mystery School approach.

SNAKE SYMBOLS

Snake symbols are found around the world. In the West, the caduceus is a common symbol denoting the medical professions, which we readily accept.

In actuality, this symbol with snakes wrapping around a center pole depicts the life force in the human body. Energy flows through the ida and the pingala—the side channels, and circles the center pole—the sushumna. In biblical terms, the snake is associated with evil and darkness; the snake tempted Eve. In the East, snakes symbolize the life force, the goddess Kundalini, in the human body, and are considered auspicious.

STAGES OF FAITH DEVELOPMENT

Originally put forth by James Fowler, based on the stages developed by Swiss philosopher and developmental theorist Jean Piaget in cognitive thinking, Lawrence Kohlberg in moral thinking, and others. Fowler posits that faith develops in individuals in stages similar to those proposed by other stage theoreticians. His work outlines the stages of Christian faith development.

Stage One (Primal or Undifferentiated Faith)

Stage Two (Mythic-Literal) – focus on pre-thought; ideas begin to form, but are not yet articulated.

Stage Three (Synthetic-Conventional) – for the most part interacts within the prevalent religion of one's upbringing, either embracing or opposing the faith, and is especially associated with the teen years.

Stage Four (Individuative-Reflective) – a stage that most individuals never reach, where an individual takes responsibility for her/his views while acknowledging the views of others.

Stage Five (Conjunctive) – reached at mid-life, if at all, the individual is aware of the transcendent.

Stage Six (Universalizing) – the position of enlightened beings.

    Note: Because there are seven chakras in the etheric body, I believe there is a seventh stage of faith development in which the soul is one with the entirety of creation.

PART THREE
Workbook for the Soul

Simple Ways to Meditate

Meditation is really quite simple. The object is to quiet the mind so that one may be in silence. For many people, the only object is to relax into a restful, non-conflicted state of awareness. For others, the object is to contact Source or God and to obtain blessings of peace, joy, and love. Some meditators like to reach a state of quiet and then pray to God. Others simply contemplate Emptiness.

Meditation is more effective if you select a special place where you intend to meditate regularly. It's especially nice to create an altar, placing on it objects of spiritual significance to you, such as rocks, statues, pictures of saints and loved ones, and perhaps some fresh-cut flowers. Lighting a candle and using incense can set the mood for meditation. Sitting at the same time every day is helpful, and selecting a seat one can maintain without moving is important. Some like to sit in lotus posture, but if this is difficult, simply use a meditation bench, a pillow, or even a chair. When you begin to meditate, you can begin with a short period, say ten to twenty minutes a sitting. As you become comfortable with it, gradually increase the time you meditate.

Whatever meditation method you choose, from the six below or from some other source, it is important to keep the spine straight. This allows the energy in your body to flow easily up and down through the various energy centers (chakras) in the body.

FIRST MEDITATION FORM – *HAMSA*, FOLLOWING THE BREATH

Breathing in through your nose, hear the natural sound of your breath entering the body as *Ham*. When you exhale, imagine the sound is *Sa*. Breathe in, breathe out, listening to the sound of your breath. *Hamsa, Hamsa.* (Some think of this as *So'ham*. Both are correct.) Keep your attention on the breath. Notice that at the end of each inhalation and exhalation, there is a slight pause; the breath momentarily stops. As your body and mind relax deeper into *Hamsa*, the points of stillness will gradually expand to longer and longer spaces between inhalation and exhalation. By staying focused on the breath, your mind will gradually cease to be drawn into thoughts. The goal is to completely still the mind. At this point, one may enter contemplation—a deep, still, and very restful place of no thought.

SECOND MEDITATION FORM – FOCUS ON A CANDLE

Light a candle. Sit gazing at the candle, spine erect. Let your mind rest in the light of the candle.

Try to still all your thoughts. If a thought comes, simply let it go and refocus your attention on the light of the candle. Do this for ten minutes, then rest in the quiet.

THIRD MEDITATION FORM – WATCHING TREES IN A GENTLE BREEZE

Find a place in your neighborhood where you will not be disturbed and there are trees. Observe the trees. Continue watching them. Notice that they are never still. Life is like that, continually changing. Our thoughts are like that, continually changing. Consider the constant change for ten minutes. Just keep watching without letting your mind wander. After ten minutes, shift your attention. Ask yourself, is there anything that is not moving? Contemplate that ineffable something that is not moving as you watch the trembling leaves on your tree, or the branches gently swaying, swaying, swaying.

I have a mental construct something like physicist David Bohm's theory of worlds within worlds within worlds, implicate order to implicate order. For me, the Divine Mother, the sacred Divine Feminine, is the source of all creation. She is Unmoving, Empty, Blissful, and simultaneously the Creator of all things. From this point of No-Thing at the spiritual heart of the universe, all things spring forth. When I meditate, I like to think of this Emptiness as simultaneously Fullness, Source of all forms. Things are constantly returning to the Source, the Divine Mother; things are constantly coming into manifestation from that same Source. Ultimately, God/Source is neither masculine nor feminine; many Eastern traditions refer to Source as feminine, while Western traditions refer to Source as masculine. Please think of God in whatever manner is most pleasing to you.

Another way I like to think of the Ineffable is as Vast Unlimited Consciousness. I think of Lord Shiva in the way the Shaivites of Kashmir think of him, as the ultimate God. Lord Shiva is always contemplating all things, utterly still and unmoving. But his consort, the feminine energy, is Shakti, and she constantly springs into action. Om, the sound of all things coming into manifestation, issues forth.

When we meditate, we can focus on the action of Shakti, coming into manifestation … the movement of the constantly changing, ever new, as in the trees. Or, we can focus on the Unchanging, the Source.

Fourth Meditation Form – Focus on a Divine Figure, a Divine Quality, or an Element

Another way to meditate is to choose a divine figure, a god or goddess, and focus on that image. Or, you may choose to focus on a quality that one finds admirable, such as love, peace, joy, or comfort. You can mentally repeat the name of the divine figure or quality to aid in your concentration. (One might say Tara, Tara, Tara. Or, love, love, love.) Still another focus for your attention might be fire, water, air, or earth. I am sure if you try these alternately in your meditations, you will discover you have an affinity for one over another. Try each of them and see what develops. You may also choose to focus on the one you least care about to see if you discern a change.

Fifth Meditation Form – Listen to Om

Another simple way of meditating is to take your seat before your altar, close your eyes, and simply listen. See if you can hear the sound of Om. Om is the word the Hindus gave to the first sound coming out of the Uncreated Source. It corresponds to Amen, the Christian word for the beginning. ("In the beginning was the Word, and the Word was God." —Gospel of St. John) Once you are attuned to the sound, you will notice it everywhere. It sounds like distant freeway traffic or the ceaseless roar of the ocean. Another similar sound is the hum of a computer. A really lovely Om sometimes sounds from Earth herself on a quiet night.

Sixth Meditation Form – Focusing on a Painful Thought

This form of meditation is subtler than the forms we have looked at so far. It recognizes what some Hindu teachers have referred to as "monkey mind." I found it useful when I was having emotional difficulty in my daily life. The idea is to take your seat in front of your altar, prepare yourself for meditation, and quiet the mind. I like to imagine that my mind is like the sky, full of broad reaches of empty space with the light of a star here and another there and so forth. If you can get the sense of spaciousness between stars, you can then attempt to focus on one star and imagine that it is your problem. You will find that "monkey mind" goes flitting off to subject after subject (star after star). Especially when one first begins to meditate, one will be aware that the mind simply will not stay quiet; it flies over the map of consciousness. You have to bring it back again and again to the problem star. In the process, you will become aware of the vastness of your inner consciousness. You can then set aside the problem star, and all the other stars in your inner sky, and simply meditate on the vast empty space that you truly are.

Observations – An Exercise in Awareness

An effective way to become more aware of the world around you as well as your feelings is to spend time journaling what you see, hear, and feel.

STEP ONE

When you begin doing this exercise, allow twenty minutes. Just sit and observe your surroundings. Are you inside? Outside? Write down what you see. Perhaps you could just jot down five simple statements: *I see a cloudy sky. The tulips in my neighbor's yard are appealing. They make me feel more cheerful. I wonder what my best friend is doing. I remember what fun we had in the city last week.*

Oops. These were not five statements about your surroundings, were they? I quickly veered off into feelings, and that made me think of my friend, which reminded me of an activity a week ago. That's okay. You can begin again: *I see a cloudy sky. The tulips ... Why did they paint their house green? I think it's going to rain. The front yard could do with a weeding.* Or, if you are intrigued with a new subject, continue writing about that.

Write for five minutes on the subject that appeals to you.

STEP TWO

Go back over what you have written. Read it aloud. Underline the words that you like—words that, for you, have energy in them.

STEP THREE

Now take the most interesting underlined word and spend five minutes writing about whatever comes up when you associate with the new word.

By now, your twenty minutes will have been used up. You certainly may continue. Or, you can put the exercise away for another day. The object of this writing exercise is to note the underlying feelings and thoughts that constantly arise in your mind. If you stay with the exercise, perhaps doing it once a day, you will find that you come to know yourself on a much deeper level and in quite an interesting way.

Questions for Self-Reflection and Journaling

The following questions, organized by age periods in the book, may be used individually or in a group. They are intended to start your thoughts flowing. You may wish to journal and/or talk them over with friends. Please expand the list to reflect additional ideas you want to explore.

CHILD OF THE CHURCH (1932–1959) ONE TO TWENTY-SIX

1. What is your earliest memory?
2. Did you attend church as a child?
3. How old were you when you knew that boys and girls were treated differently?
4. What do you remember about your ancestors?
5. Who encouraged you?
6. When you made career and life decisions, did you ever feel your choices were limited? If so, why?
7. Have you ever felt discouraged? Depressed? How have you been consoled in time of great stress?
8. Before twenty, do you remember knowing something through non-linear thought? Did you hear voices? Intuit unseen presences? Experience déjà vu or other unusual or atypical events?
9. Describe a time, if any, when you felt the presence of an angel.
10. How are you living your life purpose, as you see it?
11. Do you feel conflict between what life demands and what you feel you were meant to do?

12.How do you experience synchronicity? Do unexpected events, people, or ideas come when you least expect them? Do they guide you?
13.When did you become aware of your inner world? Or, are you?

Politics and Spirituality (1959–Summer 1982) Twenty-Seven to Forty-Nine

1.What keeps you going when you are discouraged?
2.How familiar are you with the teachings of your faith? Other traditions?
3.What is your view of hands-on-healing? Prayer? Healing at a distance?
4.Did it ever occur to you that spirituality develops the same in everyone? That there are different stages of spiritual development? What stage do you suppose you are in?
5.Where is the center of your being?
6.Is the center of your being full of light? Empty? Dark? Something in between? Are you afraid to go there?

Spiritual Community (Summer 1982–1990) Forty-Nine to Fifty-Seven

1.Have you visited another church? What was it like?
2.How do you relate to nature? Is it friendly or scary?
3.Have you practiced yoga or meditated? Do you like silence?
4.Can you remember a time when support was withdrawn? Were you stronger afterward?
5.What does empowerment mean for you?
6.Could you be at home in an ashram?
7.Travel is often described as a way to expand one's consciousness. Is that true for you? Have you been to Israel? India? Where have you traveled?
8.Are you happier in or out of relationship? Have you lived in community? Alone?
9.Has a bird or another animal ever given you a message? In what form? How did you know?
10.What would you say was the most unexpected life change you have had? How did you handle it? What kind of support did you have? From whom?
11.Write or tell (if you feel comfortable) about spiritual counseling or therapy you have had, or know about.

12.A Vision Quest is another form of spiritual retreat. Have you been on a retreat?

THE DIVINE FEMININE (1990–2006) FIFTY-SEVEN TO SEVENTY-FOUR

1. Consider how it would feel to begin life again, to pick up and move without financial or emotional support. Have you done it? What would it take to make such a change?

2.Do you feel the presence of an inner self, different from the personality others see?

3.How do you envision transcendence? Do you want to escape, or do you want to live fully in this world, in this moment? Please know there is no "right" answer.

4.Have you spent time alone in nature?

5.Have you ever made contact with a person from another culture?

6.Do you have a place of retreat?

7.For you, where and who is God?

8.What is your experience of a Divine Feminine? What is your understanding of the Goddess?

9.Summarize how your soul has informed your life. Consider intuitions, dreams, and synchronicity, events you welcomed as well as those that made you sad.

10.What one thing could you do to honor your soul? What do you plan to do next?

THE PRESENT (2007–2008) SEVENTY-FIVE

1.Are you interested in non-duality consciousness, in enlightenment?

2.Do you think your spirituality could impact or has impacted how others believe and act?

3.What do you think the Sacred Marriage within might be like?

Glossary

Absolution – A formal freeing from sin, the sacrament of reconciliation given by a Catholic priest. To pronounce free from guilt or blame.

Akashic Record – A record of every history from the beginning of time, extending into all future life, said to reveal one's past incarnations and future roles.

Ananda Spiritual Community – A combination Christian-Hindu ashram located outside Nevada City, California, founded by Donald Walters in the late 1960s, based on the writings of Paramahansa Yogananda. See Metaphysics 101.

Ashram – A secluded place for a community of spiritual devotees leading a life of simplicity and religious meditation.

Astral Projection and Out-of-Body Experiences – A phenomenon in which the consciousness of an individual seems to be outside the physical body.

Astrology – An intuitive science based on the concept of "as above, so below." Relates the placement and movement of heavenly bodies, especially planets, to what occurs in an individual's or entity's life. Can be applied to persons and nations.

Atman – Hindu, the individual soul or ego. Also, the universal soul residing in every individual.

Carl Jung – The father of transpersonal, depth psychology; writer of many books.

Chakras – Centers of spiritual energy located at seven physical centers in the human body.

Chi – Kundalini, energy, life force.

Chiropractor – A medical doctor who manipulates bones and muscles.

Dane Rudhyar – A twentieth-century astrologer and philosopher/writer. Many regard him as the father of modern astrology with its focus on the individual and psychological aspects.

Divine Feminine – The feminine counterpart to the masculine divinity, worshiped in many cultures, the original divinity.

Dreams and Visions – Dreams are the content of the unconscious mind while one sleeps; visions sometimes erupt from the unconscious during waking hours.

Ecumenical – Concerning the Christian Church as a whole; furthering the unity or unification of Christian churches.

Ecumenical Campus Minister – A minister sanctioned by two or more Christian churches to represent them on a university or college campus.

Ego – The collection of thoughts and feelings that combine to create a separate individual, sometimes referred to as the Lower Self.

Glossolalia – Speaking in tongues, an ecstatic utterance of unintelligible speech-like sounds, viewed by some as a manifestation of deep religious experience.

Great Mystery – See Holy Mystery.

Hands-on Healing – The laying on of hands resulting in the remission of pain and/or healing in body, mind, or spirit.

Harmonium – A small bellows-blown keyboard instrument developed for use by Christian missionaries in the Far East. Used for chanting before meditation.

Higher Self – A term sometimes used to denote the spiritual aspect of an individual.

Holy Mystery – That which cannot be explained, only intuited. God. Ultimate consciousness.

Holy Spirit – Catholic theology teaches there are three persons in one god: the Father (God, the Father Almighty), the Son (Jesus Christ) and the Holy Ghost (as I learned pre-1940). More recently, the Holy Ghost has been referred to as the Holy Spirit. Catholic Charismatics especially believe the Holy Spirit is feminine.

I Ching – The ancient Chinese oracle, sometimes called the Book of Changes.

Inner Self – See the Higher Self.

James Fowler – Theologian who proposed the stages of faith development.

Jiddu Krishnamurti – A twentieth-century spiritual figure, writer, and teacher.

Kibbutz – An Israeli collective settlement, especially a collective farm.

Kundalini – The sacred life force, intimately connected to the breath.

Life Force – Energy in one's body.

Lingam – The phallic symbol used in the worship of the Hindu god Shiva.

Mantra – A short, repetitive prayer.

Masonic Organizations – An international secret society having as its principles brotherliness, charity, and mutual aid.

Meditation – Deep reflection on sacred matters or objects, as a means of deepening one's connection to the spiritual and holy.

Moon Phases – Every 27 ⅓ days with reference to the stars, or once in approximately 29 ½ days with reference to the sun, the moon circles the Earth. Seen at "new moon" as barely a crescent, the moon advances through phases to full and then returns to the new phase once again. Astrological predictions are often based upon the phases of the moon. See Metaphysics 101 for additional information.

Native American Myths and Legends – Stories told by various indigenous tribes, much like fairy tales are told around the world.

Our Lady of Guadalupe – The Virgin Mary appeared at Guadalupe to a Mexican peasant; patron saint of the Americas.

Our Lady of Guadalupe Monastery – A Roman Catholic Trappist monk's place of residence and center of contemplative prayer, located in the foothills of the Pacific Coast Range, thirty-five miles west of Portland, Oregon.

Paramahansa Yogananda – An Indian spiritual master who came to the United States in the mid-twenties, founded Self Realization Fellowship, and wrote *Autobiography of a Yogi.*

Persona – That part of one's self that is presented to the world.

Planetary Influences – Astrologers track the movement of planets to determine their impact on individuals and world affairs. "As above, so below" is the philosophical foundation.

Reincarnation – The belief that we live repeated lives, soul surviving from lifetime to lifetime.

Sacrament of Reconciliation – In the Catholic Church, the rite of confession and forgiveness of one's sins.

Seer – An individual who is able to see the past and/or future. May access the personal unconscious or collective consciousness by means of many forms, including intuition, inner visions, dreams, scrying, messages from guides or channeling.

Self – Generally, the identity, character, or essential qualities of an individual. When capitalized, Self is an Indian term for Atman, the universal soul in every individual. Closely related to psychologist Carl Jung's Self, the totality of the individual of which the ego forms a small part.

Shamanic Astrology – An experiential system of astrology sourced by Daniel Giamario, based on the actual movement of heavenly bodies in the night sky. Emphasis is on location of the moon and the eastern horizon at the time of birth. The moon determines the intent of the previous lifetime and those qualities brought forth to the new life. The ascendant, the point at the eastern horizon at the time of birth, indicates the present life intent. The author is a certified shamanic astrologer, and all references to charts and astrology in the text are based on the Shamanic Astrology Mystery School approach.

Shakti – Divine power of energy worshiped in the person of the female consort of Shiva.

Shiva – Kashmiri's highest Unmanifest God, a transcendent meditating Being. In other parts of India, Shiva is the Hindu God of destruction, a member of the supreme Hindu trinity.

Shiva Lingam – Formed with a phallic symbol above and a bowl below, masculine and feminine together, depicting the marriage of Shiva and Shakti.

Snakes – Symbols of kundalini and the life force found in many cultures. See Metaphysics 101.

Soul – The immortal or spiritual part of the individual.

Soul Agenda – The soul's plan for the individual.

Spiritual Journey – The phases of development of spirituality in a soul.

Synchronicity – A term used by C. G. Jung to describe events occurring unexpectedly and seemingly unrelated, often carrying great significance. "As above, so below" is an example; the movements of the planets reflect the inner movement of the collective and personal unconscious.

Vision Quest – In Native American cultures, the search for an insight into one's life purpose, often conducted alone and under arduous circumstances.

Wedding Banns – The proclamation, generally made in church on three successive Sundays, of an intended marriage. Calls for anyone who knows of any reason why the couple should not marry to speak up.

World Brotherhood Communities – Yogananda's dream was to have enlightened spiritual communities where entire families would work, live, and pray.

Yahweh – Jewish name for God, whose name cannot be spoken.

Yogananda – See highlight, page 62

Yogic Principles – Basic tenets of Vedanta, Hinduism, and Buddhism. See text for further information.

Yurt – A Mongolian circular dwelling, usually made with skins or felt and a framework of poles.

Bibliography

Claremont de Castillejo, Irene. *Knowing Woman, A Feminine Psychology*. New York: Harper & Row, 1973.

Enya. "Marble Halls." *Shepherd Moons* album, 1991.

Fowler, James W. *Stages of Faith: The Psychology of Human Development and the Quest for Meaning*. San Francisco, Harper 1995.

Jung, C. G. *Two Essays on Analytical Psychology*, Collected Works vol. 7. Princeton, New Jersey: Princeton University Press, April 1, 1972.

Jung, C. G. *Man and His Symbols*. Garden City, New York: Doubleday, 1964.

Kohlberg, Lawrence. *Moral Stages: A Current Formulation and a Response to Critics*. S. Basel, Switzerland: Karger Publications, 1983.

Piaget, Jean. *The Construction of Reality in the Child*. New York: Basic Books, 1954.

Reinhold, Father H. A. *The Soul Afire, Revelations of the Mystics*. Garden City, New York: Image, Double Day, 1973.

Walters, Donald (Swami Kriyananda). *Christ Lives in the Holy Land and You*. Nevada City, California: Ananda Publications, 1983.

Wilbur, Ken. *The Atman Project*. Boston and London: Shambhala, 1982.

Wilhelm, Hellmut. *I Ching, The Book of Changes*. Princeton, New Jersey: Princeton University Press, 1967.

Wolski, Joann (ed.), *Women's Spirituality: Resources for Christian Development*. Paulist, 1986.

Woodman, Marion. *Leaving my Father's House.* Boston and London: Shambhala, 1992.

Yogananda, Paramahansa. *Autobiography of a Yogi.* Los Angeles, California: Self-Realization Fellowship, 1959.